D0478057

English Smart 4

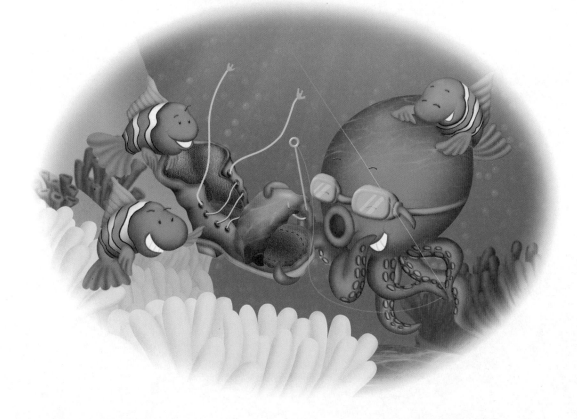

Marilyn Kennedy

Copyright © 2009 **Popular Book Company (Canada) Limited**

Printed in China

Contents

Grade 4

1 Ghosts   4-7
- *Recalling Facts*
- *Nouns*
- *Words in Context*

2 The Human Heart   8-11
- *Recalling Details*
- *Verbs*
- *Crossword Puzzle*

3 The First Heart Transplant   12-15
- *Fact or Opinion*
- *Adjectives and Adverbs*
- *Words Often Confused*

4 The Incredible Butterfly   16-19
- *Using Information*
- *Pronouns*
- *Root Words and Building New Words*

5 The Atlas   20-23
- *Recalling Details*
- *The Direct Object*
- *New Word Scramble*

6 Disasters at Sea (1)   24-27
- *The Main Idea*
- *The Indirect Object*
- *Synonyms*

7 Disasters at Sea (2)   28-31
- *Recalling Facts*
- *The Basic Sentence*
- *Synonyms*

8 Plants – Nature's Medicine   32-35
- *Recalling Facts*
- *Building Simple Sentences*
- *Antonyms*

9 Education in the Renaissance   36-39
- *Making Inferences*
- *Constructing Simple Sentences*
- *Similes*

Review 1   40-45

10 J.K. Rowling – Her Story   46-49
- *The Main Idea*
- *Prepositions*
- *Making Opposites*

11 Games and Toys of Pioneer Canada (1) 50-53
- *Drawing Conclusions*
- *Prepositions and Objects*
- *Poet's Corner*

12 Games and Toys of Pioneer Canada (2) 54-57
- *Skimming*
- *Phrases and Clauses*
- *Anagrams*

13 Medieval Castles   58-61
- *Finding Supporting Facts*
- *Adjective and Adverb Phrases*
- *Plural Forms*

14 The Thinking Organ   62-65
- *Recalling Details*
- *Conjunctions*
- *Synonyms and Antonyms*

15 The Inca Empire   66-69
- *Recalling Facts*
- *Types of Sentences*
- *Crossword Puzzle*

16 The Origins of Money   70-73
- *Remembering Facts and Making Assumptions*
- *Rules of Capitalization*
- *Haiku Poetry*

17 New France – The Beginning of Canada (1) 74-77
- *Examining Facts*   • *Punctuation*
- *New Words in Context*

18 New France – The Beginning of Canada (2) 78-81
- *Fact or Opinion*   • *Problem Sentences*
- *Word Builder Crossword Puzzles*

Review 2   82-87

Answers   89-95

Ghosts

The possibility of ghosts all around us is a scary <u>concept</u>. We picture <u>horrifying</u> shapes in <u>transparent</u> white sheets drifting above the ground making <u>eerie</u> sounds. But do ghosts actually exist?

There are various types of ghosts according to ghost specialists. The most common type is the "crisis <u>apparition</u>". This is the dead who appear to close relatives. A "tape recording ghost" is a ghost that <u>reenacts</u> an action from their time period but does not react to the living. One man reported seeing soldiers march through his house with their legs below the floor level. These ghosts were <u>oblivious</u> to the man and just walked right past him.

Some ghosts known as "cyclic ghosts" appear every year on the same day. Anne Boleyn, the beheaded wife of King Henry VIII, has been seen on December 24 in Hever Castle, Kent, her childhood home. She was seen carrying her head under her arm! Marilyn Monroe, the <u>legendary</u> movie star, has been seen on August 4, the day she died in 1962.

"Poltergeists" are mischievous ghosts. They often make loud noises and create <u>chaos</u>. Poltergeists may throw things around but they seldom hurt anyone. In one <u>documented</u> case, a poltergeist hurled a teapot across a room and just before it was to hit someone, it magically changed direction.

People troubled by ghosts can call "ghost hunters". In the 1984 film, "Ghostbusters", ghost hunters chased away ghosts with laser guns.

Recalling Facts

A. Write "T" for true if the fact is found in the passage. Write "F" for false if the statement is not found in the passage.

1. King Henry VIII's wife had her head cut off. _____

2. Poltergeists like to bother old people. _____

3. It is rare for a poltergeist to actually harm anyone physically. _____

4. If ghosts bother you, you can call a "ghost hunter". _____

5. "Ghostbusters" is the name of an actual company. _____

6. Some ghosts ignore human beings. _____

B. Draw lines to match each type of ghost with its description.

1. a crisis apparition   A. a troublemaker

2. a tape recording ghost   B. appears to relatives

3. a cyclic ghost   C. acts out a past action

4. a poltergeist   D. appears on the anniversary of its death

Using Information

C. Answer the following questions in sentence form.

1. What evidence in the story suggests that ghosts probably do exist?

    _____

    _____

2. Which type of ghost do you think is the scariest? Why?

    _____

    _____

 **Nouns**

- A **Noun** is a word that represents a person, a place, or a thing.

  Examples: 1. Judy, Mr. White, girl, teacher – are "person" nouns
  2. home, school, CN Tower, Canadian National Exhibition – are "place" nouns
  3. dog, bicycle, comb, radio – are "thing" nouns

D. Cross out the word in each list that is not a noun.

1. car, Susan, cried, museum
2. England, Rome, tired, carpenter
3. find, clothing, hat, purse
4. tears, years, fears, hears
5. behave, behaviour, student, test
6. walked, bookends, textbook, walkway
7. delicious, cake, cookies, pie
8. Atlantic Ocean, ran, teacher, parents

Common and Proper Nouns

- A **Proper Noun** is a specific person, place, or thing. It begins with a capital letter.
  Examples: John, Chicago, Air Canada Centre, Maple Avenue Public School

- A **Common Noun** is a person, place, or thing that is part of a classification.
  Examples: boy, city, arena, school – these are the general terms for the proper nouns above

E. Write the common nouns for the proper nouns.

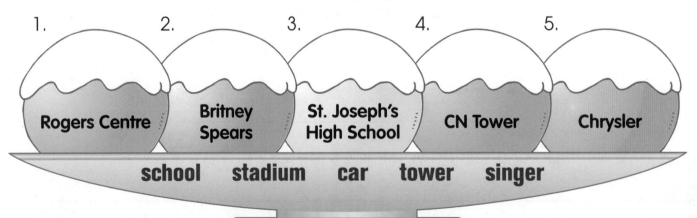

1. Rogers Centre
2. Britney Spears
3. St. Joseph's High School
4. CN Tower
5. Chrysler

school   stadium   car   tower   singer

Words in Context

- When we are trying to understand the meaning of a word that is new to us, it is helpful to read the word in its context. **Context** is the use of the word in a sentence that reveals its meaning.

F. Match the words in Column A with the definitions in Column B.

Column A	Column B
1. concept _____	A. confusion
2. horrifying _____	B. unaware
3. transparent _____	C. terrifying
4. eerie _____	D. famous
5. apparition _____	E. idea
6. reenacts _____	F. recorded
7. oblivious _____	G. strange
8. legendary _____	H. repeats
9. chaos _____	I. vision
10. documented _____	J. see-through

In the reading passage, there are 10 underlined words. Read the sentence in which each word appears and figure out its meaning.

G. Use any five words from Column A to write a sentence of your own.

1. _____

2. _____

3. _____

4. _____

5. _____

The heart is a powerful <u>involuntary</u> muscle that sends blood throughout our body. We cannot control what it does. It sends a single drop of blood around the 100,000 kilometres of blood vessels about a thousand times a day. This is an <u>incredible</u> feat for a muscle that is the size of a human fist.

The Human HEART

The heart is made up of four <u>chambers</u> – two at the top and two at the bottom. At the top, the left atrium and the right atrium collect the blood and the bottom two chambers, the ventricles, pump the blood out of the heart. It happens in one single heartbeat for the blood to go from the heart to the lungs where it loads up on oxygen and return to the heart, and then pass all over the body.

To ensure that the blood travels smoothly and <u>consistently</u>, the heart uses <u>valves</u> that open and shut with the flow of blood. The valves only open one way making sure that blood does not re-enter the chambers.

When you are ready for physical action such as running, your heart speeds up and delivers large amounts of oxygen to your legs <u>enabling</u> you to run quickly. After exercising, you may feel <u>exhausted</u> as your oxygen reserve may be used up. In a few moments, however, you will recover the oxygen needed at rest and your heart will slow down and <u>resume</u> a normal rate. The <u>typical</u> heart rate of an adult is 60 – 80 beats per minute while a younger heart would beat at a rate of 80 –100 beats per minute.

Recalling Details

A. Circle the letters of the correct answers.

1. The job of the heart is to
   A. send blood to the lungs.
   B. fill blood with oxygen.
   C. help us run quickly.
   D. send blood throughout the body.

2. The size of the human heart is about
   A. the same size as our head.
   B. the size of a fist.
   C. the size of a baseball.
   D. 5 cm in height and 2 cm in width.

3. To make sure that blood circulates smoothly, the heart uses
   A. a pacemaker.
   B. blood vessels.
   C. valves that open and shut.
   D. oxygen.

4. The valves control
   A. heartbeat.
   B. the amount of blood flow.
   C. the direction of blood flow.
   D. the amount of oxygen in the blood.

5. When you are ready for physical action, your heart delivers
   A. oxygen to your muscles.
   B. electricity to your lungs.
   C. blood to your feet.
   D. air to your lungs.

Matching the facts

B. Match the facts.

1. ventricles _____
2. 60 – 80 beats _____
3. 4 chambers _____
4. involuntary _____
5. 80 – 100 beats _____
6. open one way only _____

A. adult's heart rate
B. the atriums and the ventricles
C. type of muscle
D. the valves to prevent re-entry of blood
E. pump blood out of the heart
F. child's heart rate

 **Verbs**

- A **Verb** tells what the subject is doing (action) or describes the state of the noun (non-action).
  Examples (action): walk, run, jump, fly, sing, dance, scream
  Examples (non-action): am, is, are, was, were

C. Underline the verb in each sentence. Write "A" for action word or "N" for non-action word.

1. The birds flew high above the trees. _____

2. The children played in the park. _____

3. He is nine years old. _____

4. Where were you last night? _____

5. What time is it? _____

6. The girls sang in the choir. _____

7. He was the first to arrive. _____

8. Do not cross the street without looking both ways. _____

D. Fill in the blanks with the appropriate verbs provided.

sailed	built	took	went
stayed	flew	camped	

During the summer holidays, many students 1._____ on vacation. John 2._____ to England to visit his relatives. Susan 3._____ her uncle's boat. Paul 4._____ in the woods with his parents and 5._____ a campfire every night. Some pupils 6._____ home. They 7._____ day trips to various places.

Crossword Puzzle

E. Use the clues to complete the crossword puzzle. The words are underlined in the reading passage.

Check the meanings of these words in context.

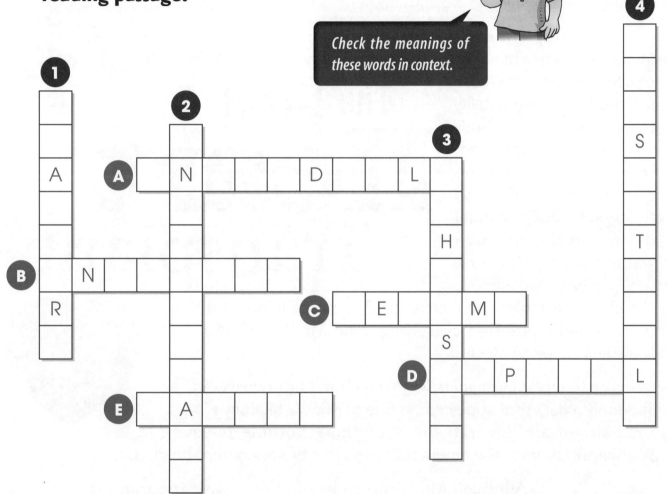

ACROSS

A. unbelievable
B. giving it the power
C. continue
D. usual
E. parts of the heart that open and shut

DOWN

1. rooms to store blood
2. acts on its own
3. tired
4. regularly, always the same

In December, 1967, in Groote Schuur Hospital in Capetown, South Africa, medical history was made. Dr. Christian Barnard performed the first successful transplant of a human heart. The patient, Louis Washkansky, received the heart of a young woman killed in a car accident.

The transplant itself was traumatic, and so were the hours immediately after the operation. There were two main concerns: The problem of possible infection and the possibility that Mr. Washkansky's body would reject the new heart. To avoid rejection, doctors gave Mr. Washkansky drugs to lessen his body's natural defence so that rejection was less likely. However, with defence weakened, the chance for infection increased. As a precaution, the doctors made sure that everything near Mr. Washkansky was sterilized or disinfected.

The First Heart Transplant

The transplant was going very well for the first two weeks. Suddenly a dark spot appeared on one of Mr. Washkansky's lungs. Dr. Barnard and his staff did everything possible to save Mr. Washkansky, but on the nineteenth day after the operation, he died.

Although Mr. Washkansky did not survive the transplant, the operation was considered a success. It paved the way for many more attempts to follow. Today, heart transplants are performed regularly. Many of those who were born with congenital heart conditions and doomed to die at an early age now live long and healthy lives, thanks to the pioneering efforts of Dr. Christian Barnard.

Fact or Opinion

- A **Fact** refers to information that is given in the passage. An **Opinion** is your interpretation of the information.

A. For each statement below, write "F" for fact or "O" for opinion.

1. A heart transplant is a delicate operation. _____

2. The first transplant made medical history. _____

3. The transplanted heart came from a car accident victim. _____

4. Everyone was worried about the time after the operation. _____

5. The possibility of infection was a major concern. _____

6. Rejection of the new heart was a possibility. _____

7. The drugs given to Mr. Washkansky were risky. _____

8. Everything around Mr. Washkansky had to be sterilized. _____

9. Mr. Washkansky died on the nineteenth day after the operation. _____

10. It is much safer to have a heart transplant today. _____

11. Congenital heart problems are serious. _____

12. Dr. Barnard is a hero. _____

Your Opinion

B. Write a response to the question giving your point of view.

Was Dr. Barnard a hero in the medical community? Give reasons.

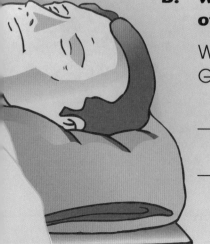

_____

_____

Adjectives and Adverbs

- We use **Adjectives** to describe nouns and **Adverbs** to describe verbs.

  The underlined words are all adjectives describing the nouns that follow them:
  the <u>little</u> boy, the <u>scary</u> story, the <u>tall</u> building, the <u>slippery</u> steps

  The underlined words are all adverbs describing the verbs next to them:
  ran <u>slowly</u>, jumped <u>high</u>, spoke <u>clearly</u>, laughed <u>hysterically</u>

C. **Underline the adjectives in the sentences. The number following each sentence tells you how many adjectives to find.**

The subject word in a sentence is not always the only noun. Remember – a noun is any person, place, or thing.

1. The excited children make for a loud party. (2)

2. The tall, husky man lifted the heavy furniture. (3)

3. The shiny new red bicycle was the perfect birthday gift. (5)

4. When the tired boy arrived home, he jumped into his warm bed. (2)

5. The expensive watch was found in the top drawer of the antique dresser. (3)

D. **Underline the adverbs in the sentences. The number following each sentence tells you how many adverbs to find.**

Adverbs often end in "ly" and they answer the questions "how", "where", "how often", and "when".

1. He had never seen such a sight. (1)

2. He moved silently and quickly like a cat. (2)

3. The athlete competed gallantly for the championship. (1)

4. The horse leaped proudly and brilliantly over the pond. (2)

5. She played bravely and courageously but lost the competition. (2)

Words Often Confused

E. Below are groups of words that are often confused because they look alike or sound similar. Circle the words that match the meanings.

Use a dictionary to check the meanings and avoid confusion.

1. belongs to it	its	it's
2. material	clothes	cloths
3. a place	here	hear
4. buy milk there	diary	dairy
5. an accomplishment	feet	feat
6. place in a race	forth	fourth
7. two of them	duel	dual
8. condition outside	whether	weather
9. pie or cake	dessert	desert
10. doesn't fit	loose	lose

F. Use the following words to make sentences to show their meanings.

1. diary   – _____

2. whether – _____

3. desert   – _____

4. forth   – _____

5. lose   – _____

The *Incredible* Butterfly

Butterflies are among nature's most beautiful creations. While their colours have always been admired, particularly by artists, they serve other purposes. Some butterflies use their colour for camouflage. They are able to blend in with tree branches or flowers that they feed on. Some butterflies use their bright colouring as a warning to predators. The Magnificent Owl butterfly has a large dot on its wing that looks exactly like an owl's eye. This tricks predators into thinking that the butterfly is a larger animal.

Most butterflies feed on the nectar of plants. They use a long mouth part called a proboscis to dip into the flowers and suck up the nectar. Some butterflies prefer to feed on rotting fruit. Butterflies are important to nature because they pollinate plants when they feed.

During its lifecycle, a butterfly goes through many changes in both body form and colour. There are four stages of butterfly life: egg, caterpillar (larva), chrysalis (pupa), and adult. After about two weeks, baby caterpillars hatch from eggs and start feeding. This stage lasts anywhere from 3 to 12 weeks, depending on the species. The pupa stage is where the caterpillar changes into a butterfly. This transformation takes about two weeks.

Butterflies are found all over the world, but the widest diversity of the species is found in tropical climates. The most familiar butterfly to North Americans is the Monarch butterfly.

Using Information

A. Write short answers to the following questions.

1. Why do artists in particular like butterflies?

    _____

2. How are butterflies important to nature?

    _____

3. How do butterflies defend themselves against predators?

    _____

    _____

B. State the four lifecycle changes of the butterfly in order.

adult   egg   pupa   larva

1. _____   2. _____   3. _____   4. _____

Further Facts

C. Fill in the blanks with the words provided.

world   **Magnificent Owl**   flowers   pupa
nectar   **Monarch**   **proboscis**

Butterflies feed on the 1. _____ of plants. They are

equipped with a 2. _____ which dips into the

3. _____ to get food. Caterpillars become butterflies in

the 4. _____ stage. Butterflies are found all over the

5. _____ . The 6. _____ butterfly has a

large dot on its wing. The 7. _____ butterfly is most familiar

to North Americans.

 **Pronouns**

- A **Pronoun** is used in place of a noun. It must agree in gender (male or female) and number with the word it is replacing.

  Singular Pronouns:
  I me mine she her hers he him his you yours it its

  Plural Pronouns:
  we us ours you yours they them theirs

D. Write the appropriate pronouns to replace the underlined nouns.

1. I drew <u>Sharon</u> a <u>birthday card</u>. _____ said _____ looked cute.

2. <u>I</u> bought this book yesterday. It is _____ .

3. Gregory called on <u>John</u> and asked if _____ could play.

4. The <u>children</u> washed their hands before _____ had lunch.

5. We let <u>them</u> use our car because _____ broke down.

6. We bought tickets for the <u>show</u> early. We didn't want to miss _____ .

7. When the new <u>students</u> arrived, the teacher asked us to help _____ .

Interrogative Pronouns

- **Interrogative Pronouns** ask questions.
  Examples: "who", "what", "whom", "which", and "whose"

E. Place the appropriate interrogative pronoun in each space provided.

1. _____ of the cars is the most expensive?

2. _____ will be joining us for dinner?

3. _____ house is this?

4. _____ are you doing this evening?

5. _____ student will be chosen to give a speech?

Root Words and Building New Words

F. **Fill in the chart below to create new words from the words given. A prefix is given for the first new word and a suffix for the second.**

> Words can be altered by adding a prefix or a suffix or by changing the form of the word.

Word	With Prefixes	With Suffixes
1. change	ex ➡	able ➡
2. print	im ➡	ing ➡
3. polite	im ➡	ness ➡
4. believe	dis ➡	able ➡
5. patient	im ➡	ce ➡
6. real	un ➡	istic ➡
7. definite	in ➡	ly ➡
8. behave	mis ➡	iour ➡
9. appoint	dis ➡	ment ➡
10. sincere	in ➡	ity ➡

G. **The root words below have been changed to make new words in the passage. Write the new word from the passage beside its root word.**

1. transform _____

2. warn _____

3. create _____

4. wide _____

5. diverse _____

6. tropics _____

7. beauty _____

8. depend _____

The Atlas

An atlas is a scale model of the earth. It helps us look at the entire earth. There are seven large land masses called continents. These include: Africa, Asia, South America, North America, Europe, Antarctica, and Australasia. The water surface of the earth is divided into five oceans: Atlantic, Pacific, Indian, Arctic, and Antarctic.

The imaginary line that circles the globe halfway between the North Pole and the South Pole is called the equator. A similar imaginary circle that runs north-south and passes through Greenwich is called the prime meridian. Lines of latitude (called parallels because they run parallel to the equator) run east-west and measure distances north and south of the equator. Lines of longitude (called meridians) run north-south and measure distances east and west of the prime meridian.

Distances on an atlas are measured in degrees ($°$). Degrees are further divided into minutes. There are 60 minutes for each degree. The equator is at $0°$ while the North Pole is at $90°$. Therefore, the distance from the North Pole to the South Pole is $180°$ in total. Similarly, the prime meridian is at $0°$ and distances east and west are between $0°$ and $180°$ in both directions for a total of $360°$ ($180°$ E and $180°$ W). Therefore, it is easy to plot an exact location on a map. Toronto, for example, is at roughly $80°$ west of the prime meridian and $45°$ north of the equator.

Recalling Details

A. Match the facts from Column A with the meanings in Column B.

Column A

Column B

1. continents _____
2. degrees _____
3. 60 _____
4. 7 of these _____
5. longitude & latitude _____
6. equator _____
7. meridians _____
8. 5 of these _____
9. parallels _____
10. prime meridian _____

A. oceans
B. located at 0° longitude
C. run parallel to the equator
D. minutes for each degree
E. measurement of longitude & latitude
F. continents
G. land masses
H. east-west/north-south lines
I. run parallel to the prime meridian
J. located at 0° latitude

Content Quiz

B. Can you list the oceans of the world?

1. _____ 2. _____ 3. _____

4. _____ 5. _____

C. Underline the seven continents. Be careful – some of these are countries, not continents.

New Zealand   Australasia   Venezuela   Australia   United States

Central America   China   Asia   Europe   Holland   Canada   Africa

South America   North America   Mexico   Antarctica

Unit 5

The Direct Object

- A **Direct Object** in a sentence is the noun that receives the action of the verb.
  Example: John kicked the soccer ball into the net.
  In this case, the object would be the "ball" since it is the noun receiving the action of the verb "kicked".

D. Underline the direct objects in the sentences below.

1. Bill took his brother to the baseball game.

2. Paul lifted the cabinet by himself.

3. The girls played tennis in the morning.

4. Don't wake me up.

5. The teacher collected the test papers.

6. The police officer arrested the thief.

7. The plane carried the passengers across the ocean.

8. In the morning, they ate breakfast and went to school.

9. She ironed her dress and polished her shoes.

10. The sun broke through the clouds and warmed the flowers.

E. Complete each sentence by placing a direct object following the verb.

1. The students in the school enjoyed _____ .

2. To make the room tidy, they cleaned _____ .

3. Her mother baked _____ .

4. The boys in the band played _____ .

5. The talented carpenter built _____ .

New Word Scramble

F. **The following scrambled words are from the reading passage. Use the definition clue to unscramble each of the words.**

1. **retine**	☐ n ☐ i ☐ ☐	the whole thing
2. **oelgb**	☐ ☐ l ☐ ☐ e	the Earth
3. **riccles**	☐ ☐ ☐ c ☐ e ☐	goes round
4. **ceaxt**	☐ x ☐ ☐ t	precise, accurate
5. **lasec**	☐ ☐ a ☐ e	the same but much smaller
6. **mirep**	p ☐ ☐ ☐ e	first, most important

Challenge: Using New Words in Sentences

G. **Choose four of the new words and use each one in a sentence.**

1. _____

   _____

2. _____

   _____

3. _____

   _____

4. _____

   _____

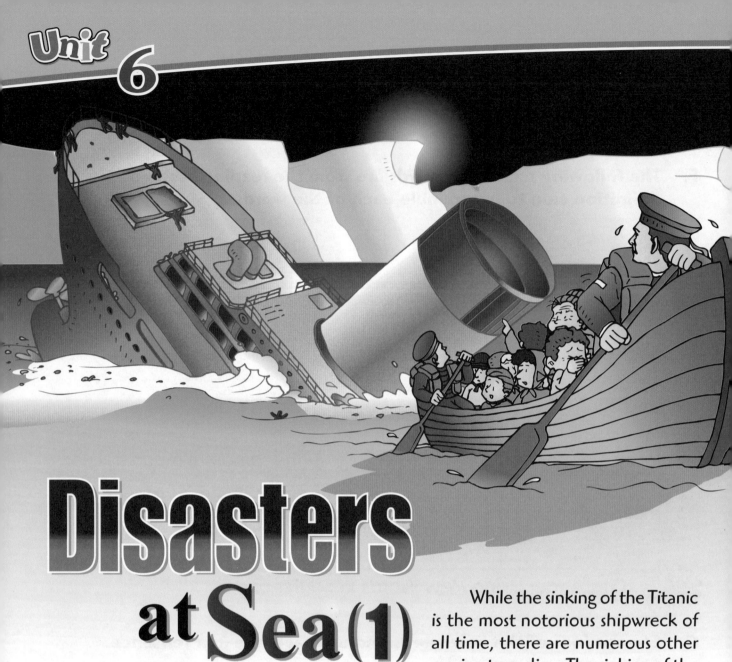

Disasters at Sea (1)

While the sinking of the Titanic is the most notorious shipwreck of all time, there are numerous other marine tragedies. The sinking of the Lusitania, the Empress of Ireland, and the Britannic are other notable disasters at sea.

On April 10, 1912, the Titanic departed on her maiden voyage from Southampton, England heading across the Atlantic to New York City. The Titanic was the most luxurious passenger liner of its time. The 2,227 passengers were to enjoy the many luxuries of the Titanic, which included a gymnasium, a heated swimming pool, elegant dining rooms, stately passenger rooms, and a grand ballroom.

Four days after leaving Southampton, a lookout by the name of Frederick Fleet spotted an iceberg approaching out of the fog. A minute later, the iceberg struck the hull of the Titanic causing severe damage. In less than three hours, the ship split in two and the bow plunged into the sea.

The ship was not equipped with enough lifeboats to carry all the passengers. When the ship was going down, many passengers were left helplessly floating in the dark, cold waters of the Atlantic. Over 1,500 died that fateful night.

The Main Idea

- The **Main Idea** of a paragraph is the basic topic being discussed.

A. Check the statement that gives the main idea of each paragraph.

1. *Paragraph One*

   A. _____ The sinking of the Titanic is the most notorious shipwreck of all time.

   B. _____ There are other notable marine disasters besides the Titanic.

   C. _____ The Lusitania is a famous ship.

2. *Paragraph Two*

   A. _____ The Titanic was on her maiden voyage.

   B. _____ The Titanic was a luxurious passenger liner.

   C. _____ The Titanic had a heated swimming pool.

3. *Paragraph Three*

   A. _____ Frederick Fleet was a lookout on the Titanic.

   B. _____ An iceberg struck the Titanic.

   C. _____ The bow of the Titanic plunged into the sea.

4. *Paragraph Four*

   A. _____ The ship did not have enough lifeboats.

   B. _____ Passengers were floating in the Atlantic.

   C. _____ Over 1,500 passengers died.

Using Facts: Your Opinion

B. Answer the following question with your opinion based on the facts of the story.

How was the Titanic poorly prepared for emergency? What extra precautions should have been taken?

_____

_____

_____

The Indirect Object

- An **Indirect Object** is to whom or what the action of the verb is directed.
  Example: He gave me the money.
  The direct object is "money" and the indirect object is "me".

C. **The underline words are the direct objects of the sentences. Circle the indirect objects.**

1. Joe is throwing his dog <u>a bone</u>.

2. She gave me <u>the instructions</u>.

3. Linda passed Cathy <u>the ball</u>.

4. The man paid the mechanic <u>$100</u>.

5. We sent him <u>the money</u> in an envelope.

6. Paul sent his mother <u>flowers</u> on Mother's Day.

7. Give him <u>a call</u> if you want to get a ride to school.

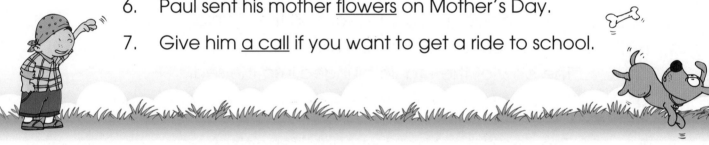

The Direct Object and the Indirect Object

D. **For each case, use the given words to compose a sentence that has a direct object and an indirect object.**

1. offered   him   ride

   _____

2. letter   sent   her

   _____

3. father   asked   reason

   _____

Synonyms

- A **Synonym** is a word that has the same meaning as another word and could be used in place of that word.

E.   For each of the eight words from the passage, circle the best synonym.

1. numerous	few many numbered most
2. tragedies	incidents occurrences disasters events
3. departed	arrived left dropped flew
4. luxurious	expensive cheap nice important
5. elegant	fancy neat tidy shiny
6. grand	small loud large necessary
7. spotted	dotted looked saw watched
8. plunged	fell floated drifted punched

F.   Pretend that you are a reporter giving an account of the sinking of the Titanic. Write your radio broadcast below.

Use as many of the new words above as you can. The first sentence is the beginning of your announcement.

This is _____ of WEBK Radio. I am reporting live from the scene of the sinking of the Titanic.

_____

_____

_____

_____

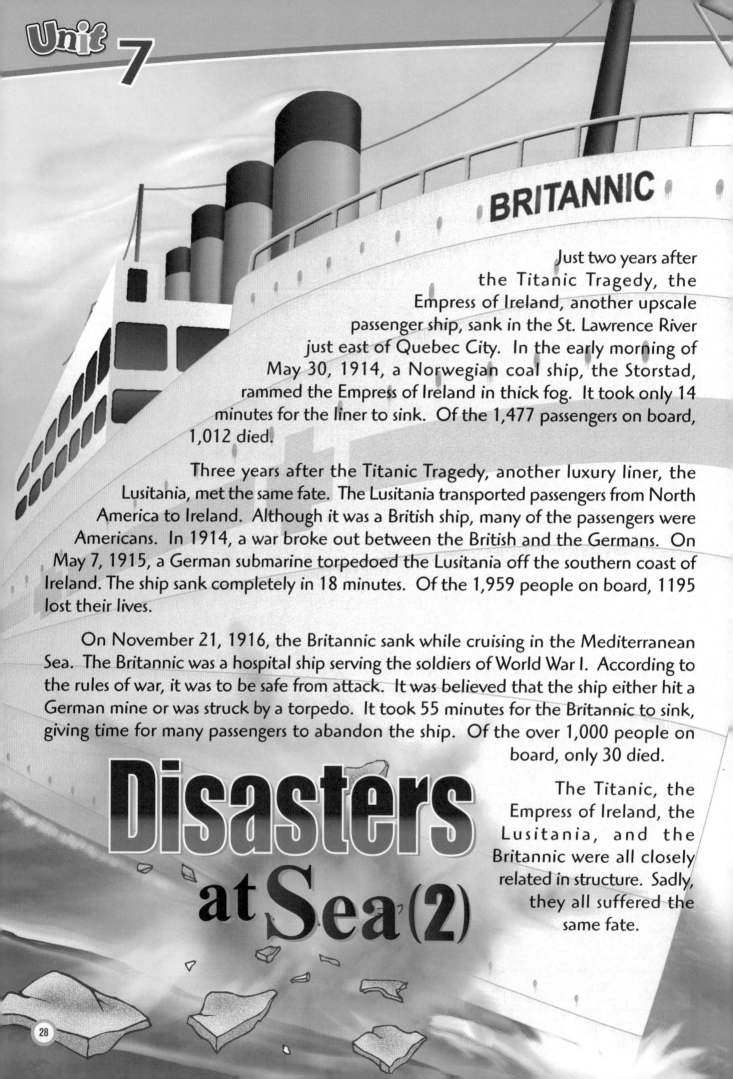

BRITANNIC

Just two years after the Titanic Tragedy, the Empress of Ireland, another upscale passenger ship, sank in the St. Lawrence River just east of Quebec City. In the early morning of May 30, 1914, a Norwegian coal ship, the Storstad, rammed the Empress of Ireland in thick fog. It took only 14 minutes for the liner to sink. Of the 1,477 passengers on board, 1,012 died.

Three years after the Titanic Tragedy, another luxury liner, the Lusitania, met the same fate. The Lusitania transported passengers from North America to Ireland. Although it was a British ship, many of the passengers were Americans. In 1914, a war broke out between the British and the Germans. On May 7, 1915, a German submarine torpedoed the Lusitania off the southern coast of Ireland. The ship sank completely in 18 minutes. Of the 1,959 people on board, 1195 lost their lives.

On November 21, 1916, the Britannic sank while cruising in the Mediterranean Sea. The Britannic was a hospital ship serving the soldiers of World War I. According to the rules of war, it was to be safe from attack. It was believed that the ship either hit a German mine or was struck by a torpedo. It took 55 minutes for the Britannic to sink, giving time for many passengers to abandon the ship. Of the over 1,000 people on board, only 30 died.

The Titanic, the Empress of Ireland, the Lusitania, and the Britannic were all closely related in structure. Sadly, they all suffered the same fate.

Disasters at Sea (2)

Recalling Facts

A. Place "T" for true statements or "F" for false ones.

1.   The Lusitania was luckier than the Titanic.   _____

2.   The Lusitania travelled from North America to Ireland.   _____

3.   Most of the passengers on the Lusitania were British.   _____

4.   An American submarine crashed into the Lusitania.   _____

5.   The Empress of Ireland sank in 1914.   _____

6.   The Empress of Ireland was a Norwegian coal ship.   _____

7.   It was foggy when the Empress of Ireland was hit.   _____

8.   The Britannic sank in the Atlantic Ocean.   _____

9.   The Britannic was a hospital ship.   _____

10. The majority of the passengers on the Britannic died.   _____

Comparing Facts

B. Complete the chart to compare the three ships.

	Empress of Ireland	Lusitania	Britannic
1. Date of sinking			
2. Type of ship			
3. Where it sank			
4. Why it sank			
5. Time taken to sink			
6. Lives lost			

The Basic Sentence

- A **Basic Sentence** is made up of two parts: the Subject and the Predicate.
- The subject contains a noun that performs the action in the sentence or is the thing being described by the predicate.

    Example: The children laughed out loud at the joke.

    The subject is "the children"; the predicate is "laughed out loud at the joke".

C. Draw a vertical line separating the subject and the predicate in each sentence below.

1. He played with his dog in the backyard.

2. His parents told him to be home by 4:30.

3. His birthday presents were hidden under the bed.

4. Melanie's best friend is Sandra.

5. Two and two make four.

6. They played hide-and-seek in the old house.

D. Match the subjects with the appropriate predicates.

Subject

1. The ballerina

2. Both his parents

3. The school team

4. Professional athletes

5. The pilot

Predicate

A. won all their games.

B. often get injured.

C. sat in the cockpit.

D. had to be on her toes.

E. went to work each day.

 **Synonyms**

E. Substitute each underlined word with an appropriate synonym.

> delicious   elegant   swiftly   depressing
> drenched   spacious   frequently   chilly
> elated   scrumptious

1. Her dress was <u>nice</u>.   _____

2. The rooms in the house were <u>big</u>.   _____

3. The food was <u>good</u>.   _____

4. She talked <u>often</u>.   _____

5. Her clothes were <u>wet</u>.   _____

6. The dessert was <u>tasty</u>.   _____

7. The children were <u>happy</u>.   _____

8. It was a <u>cold</u> night.   _____

9. It was a <u>sad</u> movie.   _____

10. He ran <u>fast</u>.   _____

F. Choose four of the words in the list and write a sentence for each.

1. _____

2. _____

3. _____

4. _____

Ancient civilizations discovered by experimenting that <u>certain</u> plants contained remedies to <u>illness</u>. They also discovered that some plants contained poisons that were often fatal. Once discovered, plants that were <u>medicinal</u> were cultivated in special gardens. This was the origin of herbal medicine as we know it today.

Plants — Nature's Medicine

There are a number of plants that produce medicines. One of the most <u>popular</u> natural medicines in wide use today is ginseng, an ancient Chinese herbal remedy, that dates back 5,000 years.

The leaves of the foxglove plant produce digitalis, which is used to treat heart conditions. It <u>helps</u> the heart beat <u>slower</u> and more regularly. The bark of the South American cinchona tree gives us quinine used to treat malaria. Quinine is also used to make tonic water. Hundreds of years ago, South American Indians discovered that chewing the leaves of the coca plant relieved pain. These leaves contain cocaine, which, in controlled doses, can be a <u>valuable</u> anaesthetic, but in large doses can be <u>deadly</u>. The deadly nightshade plant, also known as Belladonna, <u>produces</u> a drug known as atropine. This drug is used to treat stomach ailments and is also used in eye surgery. The opium poppy produces opium, which is turned into morphine, codeine, and heroine. These drugs act as pain killers when given by doctors but can be deadly if taken without control.

Some plants are used for topical treatments. The term "topical" refers to use on the outside of the body, typically on the skin. Two of the most popular plants are aloe vera and jojoba. The creams produced from these plants are sold at cosmetic counters around the world. They are believed to reduce dryness and skin damage from sunburn.

Like our <u>ancient</u> ancestors, we are discovering the <u>benefits</u> of natural medicines in our everyday life. Creams, herbal teas, and food additives are some of the <u>common</u> uses of plant medicines today.

Recalling Facts

A.   Match the facts from the reading passage with the definitions.

1.   herbal medicine   _____

2.   ginseng   _____

3.   foxglove plant   _____

4.   coca leaves   _____

5.   Belladonna   _____

6.   opium poppy   _____

7.   topical   _____

8.   aloe vera/jojoba   _____

A.   skin creams are made from these

B.   chew these to relieve pain

C.   also known as Deadly Nightshade

D.   produces powerful drugs for killing pain

E.   Chinese herbal remedy

F.   digitalis (heart drug) is made from this

G.   general term for plants used as medicine

H.   refers to outside the body

Reviewing Exact Details

B.   Place "T" for true or "F" for false beside each statement.

1.   Plant creams are sold at cosmetic counters.   _____

2.   No plants contain poison.   _____

3.   Ginseng is a recent discovery in plant medicine.   _____

4.   Cocaine is used as an anaesthetic.   _____

5.   Medicinal plants were grown in special gardens.   _____

6.   Atropine is used to treat headaches.   _____

7.   Morphine, the pain killer, is produced from opium.   _____

8.   The cinchona tree is native to North America.   _____

9.   Jojoba cream is good for the skin.   _____

Unit 8

 Building Simple Sentences

C. **Provide a suitable subject for each sentence. Try to include descriptive words to suit the predicate meaning.**

> **Example:** The excited boy jumped up and down. The word "excited" helps explain why the boy (subject) jumped up and down.

1. _____ built the swing all on his own.

2. _____ was covered in paint.

3. _____ went to the shopping mall.

4. _____ were worried about the Math test.

5. _____ flew over the fence and broke a window.

6. _____ always shares his candy.

7. _____ came first in the race.

8. _____ arrived in Canada for the first time.

D. **Compose a predicate ending for each of the incomplete sentences below. Try to include descriptive details.**

1. The fearless firefighter _____ .

2. The playful kitten _____ .

3. The entire school _____ .

4. The sad little boy _____ .

5. The entire audience _____ .

6. Most of the players on the team _____ .

Antonyms

• **Antonyms**, *unlike synonyms, are opposite in meaning.*

E. **Solve the antonym puzzle with the underlined words in the passage.**

Across

A. rare
B. unknown
C. new
D. lively
E. faster
F. health

Down

1. hurts
2. worthless
3. destroys
4. unsure
5. poisonous
6. damages

Remember, you are looking for the underlined words that are opposites of the clue words.

Education in the Renaissance

In the Renaissance Period (1500-1650), people became interested in higher education. They wanted to learn the ancient languages such as Greek and Latin and study mathematics, science, and philosophy. Many universities were founded during the 16th century.

University education was a privilege of the rich. Girls were not allowed to attend and poor people could not afford to go. A member of a wealthy family could attend university at the age of ten. He might study at various universities and since the teaching was all done in Latin, it didn't matter in which country he studied. It was not unusual for a young boy to study one year in Italy and another in France without speaking either French or Italian.

It was possible in the 16th century to complete university without learning how to read or write. Since books were handwritten, there was not enough to give one to each student. Often, only the teacher had a book. He would read to the students who would memorize what he said. Tests were oral, not written. In fact, many students finished school without ever writing a word!

For the not so wealthy, grammar schools were established in towns. They learned basic grammar and mathematics, and took part in bible study. At home, girls learned sewing, cooking, dancing, and the basics of taking care of a household. Poor children never attended school.

The Renaissance was a time when scholars did not simply accept what they were told. They conducted scientific experiments in search of answers to the mysteries of the universe. Copernicus calculated that the earth revolved around the sun but was afraid to publish his works for fear that the Church would punish him. Galileo later supported this theory. The watch, the telescope, and the submarine were some inventions of this period.

Making Inferences

- An **Inference** is an idea you get from the information provided in the reading passage that you believe could be factual or true.

A. **For each question below, give your answer based on the information you have read in the passage.**

1. If it was possible to graduate from university during the Renaissance without having learned how to read or write, how and what did pupils learn?

_____

_____

_____

2. Why were girls not allowed to go to university during the Renaissance Period?

_____

_____

_____

3. Why could the Renaissance be called "a period of curiosity"?

_____

_____

_____

4. Why was Copernicus afraid that the Church would punish him for publishing his ideas about the universe?

_____

_____

_____

 Constructing Simple Sentences

Try and find the verb first. Then build the sentence.

B. Put the words in order to construct a sentence.

1.   candles   the   cake   had   nine   it   on   birthday

_____

2.   the   around   mouse   the   chased   cat   room   the

_____

3.   son   fishing   his   went   and   the   lake   in   father   the

_____

4.   ended   school   began   when   holidays   summer   the

_____

 Using Adjectives and Adverbs

C. Fill in the blanks with adjectives and adverbs to make the passage more interesting.

Since it was a 1._____ summer day, James and Philip ran

2._____ to the 3._____ swimming pool and jumped into

the water. The 4._____ lifeguard told them not to play

5._____ in case there was an accident. Once they had cooled

off, they went to buy a 6._____ ice-cream cone. They ate their

cones 7._____ and decided that they would swim 8._____

during the summer.

Similes

- A **Simile** is a descriptive comparison between two objects that have similar qualities. These two objects are linked by the words "like" or "as". Often, animals and nature are used to form similes.

  Example: He ran like the wind.

  Here the movement of running is compared to the movement of the wind.

D. Complete the following simile comparisons.

1. He was as tall as _____ .

2. She jumped like _____ .

3. The plane flew like _____ .

4. The moon shone like _____ .

5. The actress danced like _____ .

6. The house was as large as _____ .

7. The baby was as playful as _____ .

8. The melon was as sweet as _____ .

E. Create the first part of the simile for each description below.

1. She was as _____ as a lamb.

2. He was as _____ as an ox.

3. She was as _____ as a cat.

4. He was as _____ as a pig.

5. She _____ like a tortoise.

6. He _____ like a frog.

7. She _____ like a fish.

8. He _____ like a deer.

Recalling Details

A. Place "T" for true or "F" for false in the box beside each statement.

1. There are various types of ghosts according to ghost specialists. _____

2. Crisis Apparition ghosts appear to strangers only. _____

3. Tape recording ghosts use audio equipment. _____

4. Poltergeists are mischievous ghosts. _____

5. Human beings can control whether or not their heart beats. _____

6. The heart has five chambers. _____

7. A child's heart would beat 80 to 100 times per minute. _____

8. Christian Barnard was the first heart transplant recipient. _____

9. The first heart transplant recipient died 19 days after the operation. _____

10. Some butterflies use their colour as a camouflage. _____

11. Most butterflies feed on nectar. _____

12. There are three stages of the butterfly's life cycle. _____

13. The earth's surface is made up of 7 large land masses. _____

14. The water surface of the earth is divided into 6 oceans. _____

15. Grid lines on a map that run east-west are called lines of longitude. _____

16. Lines of longitude are called meridians. _____

17. The equator divides the earth in halves. _____

B. Circle the letters of the correct answers.

1. The Titanic was thought to be
   A. the fastest ship.　　B. the largest ship.　　C. unsinkable.

2. The Titanic left Southampton to go to
   A. Boston.　　B. New York.　　C. Montreal.

3. The number of people that died on the Titanic was
   A. over 1,500.　　B. fewer than 1,000.　　C. over 2,200.

4. The Lusitania transported passengers between
   A. England and France.　　B. England and Germany.　　C. Ireland and America.

5. The Lusitania sank because
   A. it hit an iceberg.　　B. it was torpedoed.　　C. it had a faulty engine.

6. The Britannic was a
   A. hospital ship.　　B. cargo ship.　　C. battleship.

7. A popular herbal medicine used today is
   A. tree bark.　　B. rice.　　C. ginseng.

8. Topical treatment refers to plants that help heal the
   A. outer body.　　B. inner soul.　　C. vital organs.

9. In the Renaissance Period, women were not allowed to
   A. get married.　　B. have children.　　C. go to university.

10. In the 16th century, one could finish university without
    A. being able to write.　　B. going to school.　　C. speaking French.

11. In the Renaissance Period, scholars were interested in
    A. plant life.　　B. science.　　C. leisure.

Review 1

 Nouns and Verbs

There may be more than one verb or noun in a sentence. Also, the noun does not have to be the subject.

C. Underline the nouns and put parentheses ( ) around the verbs in the following sentences.

1. She likes eating ice cream on a hot day.

2. He tripped over his shoelace and fell down the stairs.

3. The boys and girls played in the same yard.

4. Jim, John, and Sam walked to school together.

5. Linda is five years older than Susan.

6. The neighbours held a garage sale on their street.

7. Winter is a long and cold season.

8. Time is wasted when we do nothing.

9. The clock struck three and the school bell rang.

 Adjectives and Adverbs

Adjectives describe nouns while adverbs describe verbs.

D. Underline the adjectives and circle the adverbs in the sentences below.

1. The blazing sun sank slowly in the West.

2. The happy child opened her birthday present quickly.

3. Slowly but surely, the skilled skiers slipped down the hill.

4. Karen, a tall girl, was chosen immediately for the basketball team.

5. He ran swiftly between the stone obstacles on the sandy beach.

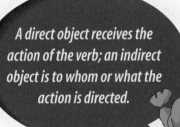

A pronoun is used in place of a noun or to refer to a noun used previously in a sentence.

 Pronouns

E. Fill in the blanks in the following sentences with pronouns.

1. Lisa's parents watched him/her _____ playing.

2. He/She _____ likes to eat her lunch outdoors.

3. John told we/me _____ about his problem.

4. They/We _____ bought themselves ice cream cones.

5. Susan asked when she/her _____ would be allowed to go home.

 Direct and Indirect Objects

A direct object receives the action of the verb; an indirect object is to whom or what the action is directed.

F. Underline the direct object and circle the indirect object in each sentence.

1. He gave me the ball.

2. We sent Grandma a postcard.

3. The parents gave their son a new bicycle.

4. The quarterback threw the running back the ball for a touchdown.

5. The teacher gave us one more chance to finish our work.

 The Subject and Predicate

The subject is the performer of the action or is the thing described by the predicate.

G. Match each subject with a suitable predicate.

1. The Toronto Maple Leafs _____   A. could not stop in time.

2. The driver _____   B. can be dangerous if you fall.

3. Skiing _____   C. both made the swim team.

4. Bob and Billy _____   D. practised in the old arena.

5. People in Nunavut _____   E. prepare for a long and cold winter.

New Words from the Reading Passages

H.   Match the words from the passages with the definitions.

1. origin   _____   A.   unaware, no knowledge of

2. transparent   _____   B.   the beginning of, starting point

3. eerie   _____   C.   all the time, regularly

4. oblivious   _____   D.   disorder, confusion

5. chaos   _____   E.   expensive, tasteful, luxurious

6. consistently   _____   F.   well-known, well-liked

7. resume   _____   G.   continue, carry on

8. elegant   _____   H.   left, went away

9. departed   _____   I.   see-through

10. popular   _____   J.   scary, weird, haunted

Words Often Confused

I.   Choose the correct word for the meaning of each sentence.

1. She wrote in her dairy/diary _____ daily.

2. He came forth/fourth _____ in the race.

3. She accomplished an amazing feet/feat _____ .

4. He couldn't decide weather/whether _____ or not to play.

5. The enemies fought a duel/dual _____ .

6. He was sitting so far away he couldn't here/hear _____ .

Forming New Words

J. **Add a prefix or suffix to each of the words to make a new word.**

1. arrange   _____
2. organize   _____
3. view   _____
4. connect   _____
5. mind   _____
6. appoint   _____
7. satisfied   _____
8. create   _____
9. belief   _____
10. care   _____
11. rely   _____
12. depend   _____
13. distant   _____
14. happy   _____
15. prior   _____
16. known   _____

Descriptive Language

K. **Change the words in parentheses to the more descriptive words from below.**

| drenched | hilarious | bitterly | antique |
| kind | spacious | delicious | pelting |

1. Dinner was (good) _____ .

2. The movie was (very funny) _____ .

3. The winter night was (very) _____ cold.

4. The (nice) _____ person helped the lady.

5. They were (wet) _____ from the (amount of) _____ rain.

6. The (big) _____ room was filled with (old) _____ furniture.

J.K.Rowling –
Her Story

The success of the Harry Potter series of novels for adolescents is a modern day phenomenon. Millions of copies have been sold worldwide. When its writer, J.K. Rowling, made a personal appearance in Toronto at the SkyDome, she drew the largest crowd ever recorded for a public reading session.

J.K. Rowling is now enjoying fame and wealth but it wasn't always that way. When she began to write the first Harry Potter book, she was a single mother of an infant daughter living on social assistance. She lived in a tiny rented apartment in Edinburgh, Scotland. She spent time in a local cafe where she wrote her first story, *Harry Potter and The Sorcerer's Stone*. This novel completely changed her life.

As a child, J.K. Rowling loved English Literature. She wrote her first real story at the age of 6. It was then that she decided that she wanted to become a writer. She thought writing would be the best occupation because she would be getting paid to do something she enjoyed.

J. K. Rowling isn't absolutely sure where she gets the ideas for the Harry Potter stories. The odd names for her characters come from a variety of sources. Some of her characters are loosely based on real people that she knows. However, once she starts to develop the characters, they become different from their source. The Potter stories are not based on Rowling's life, although most authors put a little of themselves into their writing.

Through the Harry Potter series, J.K. Rowling has been credited with increasing the interest in reading for children around the world.

The Main Idea

A. **Circle the letter of the most appropriate statement that gives the main idea of each paragraph.**

Paragraph One

A. J.K. Rowling enjoys writing.

B. J.K. Rowling is a popular author.

C. Harry Potter novels are interesting.

D. Harry Potter is an interesting character.

Paragraph Two

A. J.K. Rowling is wealthy.

B. J.K. Rowling was a poor author.

C. J.K. Rowling drinks coffee.

D. Harry Potter saved her life.

Paragraph Three

A. Six-year-olds can be writers.

B. Write when you're young.

C. J.K. Rowling loved literature.

D. Don't write unless you get paid.

Paragraph Four

A. J.K. Rowling writes about people that she knows.

B. The characters in her books are sometimes based on real people.

C. Her novels are based strictly on her life.

D. Her characters are all made up.

Your Opinion

B. **Answer the question.**

Why is J.K. Rowling credited with changing the reading habits of children around the world?

_____

_____

_____

Prepositions

- A **Preposition** helps connect a noun or pronoun to another part of the sentence. It also connects a verb to other words in the sentence.

    Example: The students in the class read quietly.

    The word "in" connects the subject, students, to the class. Now we know that they are the students from the class.

    Example: He placed his hat on the hook.

    The word "on" connects the verb "placed" to the word "hook", which is where the hat is placed.

C. Choose eight prepositions and use each to create a sentence. After each sentence, place "N" if the preposition connects a noun to other words and "V" if it connects a verb to other words.

after	down	into	under	inside	near	without
until	beside	at	above	around	below	of
on	for	from	before	among	about	with

1. The children played baseball in the yard.   (V)

2. _____ (   )

3. _____ (   )

4. _____ (   )

5. _____ (   )

6. _____ (   )

7. _____ (   )

8. _____ (   )

9. _____ (   )

Making Opposites

D. Add the proper prefixes to the words to make the opposites.

1. un/im   _____ prepared

2. dis/un   _____ appointed

3. dis/un   _____ fair

4. un/im   _____ proper

5. im/un   _____ possible

6. un/dis   _____ honour

7. un/dis   _____ approve

8. dis/un   _____ likely

9. dis/un   _____ happy

10. in/un   _____ complete

11. dis/un   _____ necessary

12. im/un   _____ perfect

Building Vocabulary

E. Change the word in parentheses in each sentence to a form that fits the sense of the sentence.

Example: John is (give) _____ away his bicycle.

You would place the word "giving" in the space, which is a form of the word "give" in parentheses.

1. Show (kind) _____ towards others.

2. It was (terrible) _____ cold outside.

3. Be (care) _____ when you go swimming.

4. They were studying the (move) _____ of the earth.

5. The wedding was followed by a (celebrate) _____ .

6. He was very (help) _____ when he was needed.

7. It was a (beauty) _____ morning with the sunshine.

8. She could not find the (solve) _____ to the problem.

The toys children play with today are often highly technical and electronic, and involve the use of a computer. The children of pioneer Canada, however, did not have such advanced toys and games as these. Instead, they relied on making their own toys and creating interactive games that involved simple physical action.

Although their toys were simple, pioneer children were never bored. After a hard day's work helping their parents on the homestead, they looked forward to free time for play. Many of their favourite games like blind man's bluff and hide-and-seek are still played today. A rope tied to a tree made a perfect swing and a plank over a

Games and Toys of Pioneer Canada (1)

saw-horse made an ideal seesaw. In playgrounds of today, the swing and the seesaw are still very popular. These playground favourites are perhaps better made today but are no more enjoyable than they were for pioneer children.

Nature provided not only the material for making toys but also the toy itself. A weeping willow tree beside a creek was an exciting toy. Children would swing on a willow branch over the creek and let go, creating a splash. This activity was a perfect way to cool off on a hot summer day.

Horseshoe pitching was one of the most popular games all across Canada. It was not only a game for children. Adults took this game very seriously and competitions between neighbours and towns were common.

Drawing Conclusions

- A **Conclusion** is an opinion reached after considering facts and details.

A. Draw conclusions for the following questions.

1. Why were pioneer children happy to have simple toys?

_____

_____

2. Why would swinging from a tree over a creek be so much fun for pioneer children?

_____

_____

3. What facts in the story suggest that pioneer children were always busy?

_____

_____

4. What would lead you to believe that horseshoe pitching was a very important pastime in pioneer days?

_____

_____

5. How can nature and the use of one's imagination result in creating fun and interesting games?

_____

_____

Recalling Facts

B. Explain how you would make the following toys. Be sure to mention all the materials you would need.

1. a seesaw   _____

2. a swing   _____

 Prepositions and Objects

- A **Preposition** is often followed by a noun acting as object of the preposition.
  Example: He climbed over the fence.
  The preposition is "over" and "fence" is the noun, object of the preposition.

C. Underline the object of the preposition in each sentence.

1. The clouds flew across the sky.

2. In the morning, she went jogging.

3. They ate lunch beside the pond.

4. Within the school, there are many different students.

5. After the rain, the road was slippery.

D. Finish each rhyme by adding the appropriate object of the preposition.

1. The cow jumped over the _____ .

2. Little Miss Muffet sat on her _____ .

3. Jack and Jill went up the _____ .

4. Humpty Dumpty sat on a _____ .

5. Hickory Dickory Dock, the mouse ran up the _____ .

E. Create sentences, using these prepositions and objects.

1. _____ around the block.

2. _____ beneath the ground.

3. After lunch, _____ .

4. _____ into the closet.

5. Before school began, _____ .

6. _____ between the houses.

Poet's Corner

- When the 1st and 2nd lines of a poem rhyme, and the 3rd and 4th lines rhyme, the poem is following an "aa/bb" rhyming scheme. Lines of poetry placed together form a verse.

    Example: The morning sun shines <u>bright</u>
    Day replaces <u>night</u>
    Flowers awake from their <u>sleep</u>
    Birds sing cheep, <u>cheep</u>.

F. Use the "aa/bb" rhyming scheme to compose a two-verse poem or two one-verse poems.

Do you want to become a poet? Here are some rhyming words to work with.

high/try/sigh/fly/sky/sly   long/song/strong   ate/plate
mouse/house   feed/need/seed

Title: _____

_____

_____

_____

_____

free/tree/see/sea/me

same/name/tame/came/fame

Title: _____

_____

_____

_____

_____

Games and Toys of Pioneer Canada (2)

Since there were no manufactured toys available to pioneer children, they had to be very creative when it came to making their own toys. A simple ball was made out of a stuffed pig's bladder, which was sturdy enough to be kicked around the field without breaking open. The name "pigskin" which referred to this type of ball is a term still in use today. Hoop rolling was also a popular game. An iron or wooden hoop and a stick were all that was needed. The challenge was to see who could keep it rolling the longest.

With Canadian winters being so cold, indoor games were important. The pioneer children did not have malls, movie theatres, or skating rinks for shelter from the winter weather. Shadow picture making was a family favourite. They would seat a family member in front of a candle and hold up a sheet of paper. A silhouette was created and then traced.

Many games were useful in helping boys and girls prepare for adult life. Girls made rag dolls and sewed clothing. These were not as perfect in form as today's Barbie but were enjoyed just as much, and valuable skills were learned. Boys went hunting and fishing with their fathers. Making a strong fishing rod out of a tree branch was an important skill. Aside from putting food on the table, fishing was a relaxing summer pastime for a pioneer boy. Boys were skilled with knives and learned the art of carving, which was useful for making toys for their younger brothers and sisters. A pocketknife could be used to make a sturdy bow and arrow set or wooden soldiers.

Pioneer life was not as fast-paced as life today. Without automobiles, travel was rare and much time was spent around the home. Therefore the pioneer children had to find things to do to occupy their time. Even though they were without television and radio, life was never dull. There was always work to do, fields and streams to play in, and the creative art of toy making to keep them busy.

Skimming

A. **Re-read the passage quickly, taking in as many facts as you can. Once you have finished that second reading, answer the questions below. Try to answer with the exact facts from the passage.**

1. What was a ball made from? _____

2. What was the name of this type of ball? _____

3. What game was played with a hoop and a stick? _____

4. In the game of shadow making, what was traced? _____

5. What toy did girls make? _____

6. What was used to make a fishing rod? _____

7. Why was travel rare in pioneer days? _____

Fact or Opinion

- A **Fact** refers to information that is given exactly from the passage. An **Opinion** is your interpretation of the information in the passage.

B. **For each statement below, place "F" for fact or "O" for opinion in the space provided.**

1. Pioneer children were never bored. _____

2. Pioneer boys relaxed when they went fishing. _____

3. Girls could be creative when making their dolls. _____

4. A pocketknife could be used to make wooden soldiers. _____

5. There were no manufactured toys available to pioneer children. _____

 Phrases and Clauses

- A **Phrase** is a group of words forming part of a sentence. It often begins with a preposition, followed by a noun.

- A **Clause** is a group of words that include a subject and a verb.
  Example: <u>At the age of seven</u>, Pat already played the piano well. (phrase)
  <u>When she was seven</u>, Pat already played the piano well. (clause)

C. Check if the underlined group of words in each sentence is a phrase or a clause.

P   C

1. <u>In front of the stage</u> sat the judges.   ____   ____

2. I was surprised <u>that she failed the test</u>.   ____   ____

3. <u>During the game</u>, the fans cheered wildly.   ____   ____

4. The toys <u>in the box</u> belong to Jenny, not Katie. ____   ____

5. She was moved to tears <u>when we offered to help her</u>. ____   ____

6. <u>Because he was the first to arrive</u>, he got the best seat. ____   ____

7. <u>Because of the heavy rain</u>, the baseball game was called off. ____   ____

8. <u>When we arrived at the stadium</u>, all the good seats were taken. ____   ____

D. Complete the sentences with suitable phrases or clauses.

1. The boy _____ hit a grand slam.

2. After _____ , they all went to Sam's place.

3. She bought this necklace because _____ .

4. The books _____ belong to our teacher.

5. During _____ , we went to buy pop and popcorn.

6. Although _____ , we chose him to be our captain.

Anagrams

- An **Anagram** is a word in which the letters can be moved around to form another word.

  Example: The letters in "tries" can be rearranged to make "tires".

E. Make new words using the clues. Do not add letters.

rats	look up to the sky	1. _____
ocean	boat that is easy to tip	2. _____
top	cooking utensils	3. _____
cheap	soft fruit	4. _____
could	holds the rain	5. _____

Homophones

- **Homophones** are words that sound the same but are spelled differently and have different meanings.

F. Complete the crossword puzzles with homophones of the words across.

1. clothing

w h e r e

2. ears

h e r e

3. tossed

t h r o u g h

4. horse's ____

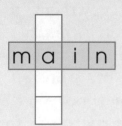

m a i n

5. no strength

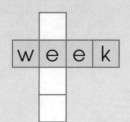

w e e k

6. wind

s a l e

Medieval castles were built to house the local lords and their families. Inhabitants of the castles usually had their own apartments. Castles were equipped with a nursery, a brewhouse, a school, a chapel, a library, many bedrooms, and an elegant dining room. The dining room was furnished with a grand table for entertaining important guests. Fireplaces were numerous throughout a castle and provided the main source of heat for the apartments. Bedrooms had huge four-poster beds with soft feather pillows and thick curtains to prevent drafts.

Medieval Castles

The main purpose of a castle was protection. A lord who owned a large amount of land would lease the land out to farmers who would pay him farm produce as rent. He would offer protection against enemy attacks. In the case of an attack, villagers would gather within the castle walls and help defend the castle against invaders. As a result, villages were established near the castle.

Castles were expensive to run. It would cost millions of dollars by today's standards to build and maintain a castle. A noble in medieval times would have an income of about £1,000 or $2,500 per year. An ordinary working person might earn the equivalent of one dollar a year. But castle owners had huge expenses. They often employed 300 people to perform various tasks.

In the late 1500's, when battles became large-scale events, castles were not needed. Today, many castles in Europe have been converted into hotels and guesthouses. Many castles are for sale by owners who cannot afford to occupy them. In fact, castles can be purchased for a lot less than you would expect. The real cost comes once you move in and try to pay for the household expenses.

Finding Supporting Facts

A. For each case, place a check mark beside the information that best proves the statement given.

1. Medieval castles were not built for local people.

   A. _____ Castles were too far from the village.

   B. _____ Castles were occupied by lords and ladies.

   C. _____ Local people did not like castles.

2. Castles were well equipped.

   A. _____ There were high walls around the castle.

   B. _____ A castle had a library, ballroom, nursery, and a school.

   C. _____ Castles were used for defence against invaders.

3. The castle was used for protection.

   A. _____ Villagers hid inside the castle when being attacked.

   B. _____ Only the lord of the castle was protected.

   C. _____ The castle was evacuated during an attack.

4. It cost a great deal of money to run a castle.

   A. _____ Some castles employed 300 people.

   B. _____ Castles needed many repairs.

   C. _____ Castle furniture was expensive.

5. Noblemen were wealthy in medieval times.

   A. _____ Nobles worked very hard to earn money.

   B. _____ Local farmers paid heavy taxes.

   C. _____ A nobleman could have an income of £1,000 a year.

6. Fewer castles were being built.

   A. _____ There were not enough building materials.

   B. _____ There were no workers to build the castles.

   C. _____ Battles were large-scale events and fought on battlefields.

Adjective and Adverb Phrases

- A **Phrase** is a group of words without a verb. It often begins with a preposition.
  An **Adjective Phrase** describes a noun.
  An **Adverb Phrase** describes a verb.

Example: The gift in the box was made in Italy.

The adjective phrase "in the box" describes the noun; the adverb phrase "in Italy" tells where the gift was made.

B. Underline the adjective phrase in each sentence and place parentheses ( ) around the adverb phrases.

1. In the morning, the sun rose over the cliffs.

2. The teacher of grade four sat at his desk.

3. The dog in the kennel barked loudly.

4. She hid under the desk.

5. He ran up the road and down the hill.

6. Under the rainbow, you will find a pot of gold.

Look for the prepositions first.

CHALLENGE

C. Create sentences with adjective or adverb phrases using the given prepositions provided.

1. (over) _____.

2. (beneath) _____.

3. (behind) _____.

4. (of) _____.

5. (in) _____.

6. (across) _____.

Plural Forms

D. Circle the correct plurals and complete the rules of spelling in your own words.

1. **knife** – knifes / knives   2. **life** – lives / lifes
3. **half** – halves / halfs

Rule: For some words ending in "f" or "fe", change _____ .

4. **army** – armies / armys   5. **family** – family / families
6. **city** – citys / cities

Rule: For words ending in "y" with a consonant before the "y", drop
_____ .

7. **journey** – journies / journeys   8. **key** – keys / keies
9. **valley** – valleies / valleys

Rule: For some words ending in "y" with a vowel before the "y", add
_____ .

CHALLENGE

E. Form the plurals of the following words.

1. goose _____   2. child _____
3. foot _____   4. man _____
5. tooth _____   6. mouse _____

7. What do these words have in common in terms of their plural form?

   sheep   aircraft   deer   moose   grass   salmon

_____

Of all the <u>organs</u> in the human body, none is more <u>vital</u> than the brain. The brain is what gives us our identity. The acts of making decisions, solving problems, and identifying objects are all the direct responsibility of the brain.

The human brain stops growing when we are about six or seven years of age. When its growth is complete, the brain weighs about 3 kilograms. The brain is the most <u>amazing</u> and <u>complex</u> object we know. It takes care of the <u>creative</u> things we do such as painting pictures, writing stories, designing buildings, or building computers. The brain processes information from all around us. When a traffic light turns red, we know not to cross the street or when a dog growls at us, we know to keep away. Much of this information is <u>stored</u> in our memory. The brain also controls all our <u>emotions</u>.

The largest part of the brain is called the cerebrum, which controls the muscles and processes sight, sound, tastes, and smell messages. The left side of the cerebrum controls the right side of the body and the right side controls the left side of the body. The left side is <u>dominant</u>, which accounts for why most people are right-handed. Below the cerebrum is the cerebellum that controls balance and co-ordination. Near the cerebellum is the medulla oblongata that controls bodily functions such as breathing, swallowing, and vomiting. The hypothalamus controls our emotions, particularly anger and <u>fear</u>, and it controls body temperature, hunger, and thirst. The brain is also directly <u>connected</u> to our central nervous system.

The Thinking Organ

The brain has always been a <u>mystery</u> to mankind. We only know the basics of how it works. The more we study the brain and its <u>function</u>, the more we realize how complicated it is.

Recalling Details

A. **Fill in the blanks in the passage below with the appropriate words.**

cerebellum   nervous   left   cerebrum   organ
hypothalamus   growing   process   memory   emotions

The human brain is the most important 1._____ in the body.
When we reach the age of six, the brain stops 2._____ . The main
function of the brain is to 3._____ information. Much of this
information is stored in our 4._____ . The brain also controls our
5._____ such as happiness and sadness. The 6._____
is the biggest part of the brain. It is above the 7._____ . Most
people are right-handed because the 8._____ side of the brain is
dominant. The 9._____ controls emotions and body temperature.
The brain is connected to our central 10._____ system.

B. **Match the facts from the passage with the descriptions or definitions.**

1. 3 kilograms   _____   A. controls hunger and thirst
2. cerebrum   _____   B. controls right side of body
3. left side of brain   _____   C. controls balance and co-ordination
4. cerebellum   _____   D. largest part of the brain
5. medulla oblongata   _____   E. weight of the brain
6. hypothalamus   _____   F. controls bodily functions

Your Opinion

C. **Why do you think that the brain is still a mystery to scientists today?**

_____

_____

Conjunctions

- **Conjunctions** are words that join words, phrases, and clauses in a sentence.

    Example 1: He ran and jumped. (joining words)

    Example 2: I will see you after the game or during lunch. (joining phrases)

    Example 3: It was a warm day although the sky was cloudy. (joining clauses)

    Example 4: Paul walked home. He met a friend. → Paul walked home and met a friend. (joining two sentences into one)

D. Complete the sentences below with appropriate conjunctions.

> because   while   until   so   unless
> and   or   but   if   since

Use each of the conjunctions above once only.

1. Peter _____ Roger were on the same team.

2. She won't wear it _____ it fits properly.

3. He has been tired ever _____ he caught a cold.

4. She was happy _____ it was her birthday.

5. Either Sheila _____ Martha will say the speech.

6. He waited in the car _____ she went shopping.

7. He made the decision _____ it was not popular.

8. She will help you _____ you help yourself.

9. They made the rules _____ it was their responsibility.

10. She couldn't wait _____ the holidays came.

Synonyms and Antonyms

- A **Synonym** is a word that means the same as another word.
- An **Antonym** is a word that means the opposite of another word.

E. **Use the underlined words in the reading passage to complete the following word puzzles.**

1. simple (antonym)

2. main (synonym)

3. boring (antonym)

4. body parts (synonym)

5. solution (antonym)

6. feelings (synonym)

7. linked (synonym)

8. courage (antonym)

9. unimportant (antonym)

10. imaginative (synonym)

11. use (synonym)

12. saved (synonym)

F. **Choose two words from the puzzles above and write two sentences of your own.**

Try to be creative.

1. _____

_____

2. _____

_____

Between 1200 and 1535 AD, the Inca built the largest empire in South America, extending from the Equator to the Pacific coast of Chile. The Inca were fierce warriors with a strong and powerful army. However, their prosperity came to a tragic end when the Spanish conquerors took over their territory.

The architecture of the Inca cities still amazes and puzzles most scientists. The Inca built their cities and fortresses on highlands and on the steep slopes of the Andes Mountains. Stone steps lead up to the top of the cities. The stone blocks weighing several tons are fit together so tightly that not even a razor blade can fit through them. Their homes were made from the same stone material and had grass rooftops.

The Inca developed sophisticated drainage systems and canals to expand their crop resources. They also reared llamas for meat and transportation. There were more than enough resources for everyone. The Inca had a good road system to connect the villages too. The roads were lined with barriers to prevent people from falling down the cliffs.

The Inca were not only fierce warriors but they also had a violent punishment system. People who committed theft would have their hands cut off or eyes taken out. Those who committed murder would be thrown off a cliff or hung up to starve to death.

The Inca Empire

Ironically, though, the 40,000-member army of the Inca was destroyed by a 180-member Spanish army led by Francisco Pizarro. The warriors of the Inca were simply no match for the Spanish guns. By 1535, the Inca society was completely wiped out. Now, only a few traces of Inca ways remain in the native culture as it exists today.

Recalling Facts

A. Decide if the following statements are true "T" or false "F".

1. The Inca Empire existed for more than 300 years. _____

2. The Inca were good warriors. _____

3. They had a legal system to uphold law and order. _____

4. The Spanish defeated the Inca warriors because they had stronger weapons. _____

5. The Inca used llamas for transportation. _____

6. The Inca architecture is like a puzzle to scientists of today. _____

7. An Inca thief would be sentenced to imprisonment. _____

8. Canals were dug for irrigation. _____

9. The common people dwelled in grass huts. _____

10. The nobles lived on the highlands while the common people lived along the coast. _____

Your Opinion

B. Answer the questions.

1. Why does the architecture of Inca amaze most scientists?

   _____

   _____

2. Do you agree to the Inca punishment system? Why?

   _____

   _____

3. How could the Spanish army defeat the Inca warriors?

   _____

   _____

Types of Sentences

- There are four main types of sentences:

  1. **Declarative** – simply makes a statement and ends with a period.
     Example: John caught the ball.

  2. **Interrogative** – asks a question and ends with a question mark.
     Example: What time is it?

  3. **Imperative** – gives a command or makes a request and ends with a period.
     Example: Answer the telephone.

  4. **Exclamatory** – expresses emotion or strong feelings and ends with an exclamation mark.
     Example: Help me, I'm falling!

C. Punctuate each of the following sentences and state the type of sentence in the space provided.

Don't forget to punctuate the sentences.

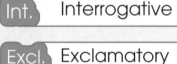

| Decl. | Declarative | Int. | Interrogative |
| Imp. | Imperative | Excl. | Exclamatory |

1. Look out   _____

2. Stop before it's too late   _____

3. The sun is shining today   _____

4. Whose birthday is it   _____

5. Wash your hands before dinner   _____

D. Compose your own sentences.

1. Declarative: _____

2. Interrogative: _____

3 Imperative: _____

4. Exclamatory: _____

Crossword Puzzle

E. Complete the crossword puzzle with the words from the passage.

Across
A. deprived of food
B. the art of building
C. surprises
D. join
E. castles

Down
1. fighters
2. advanced
3. extremely sad
4. violent and angry
5. signs of existence

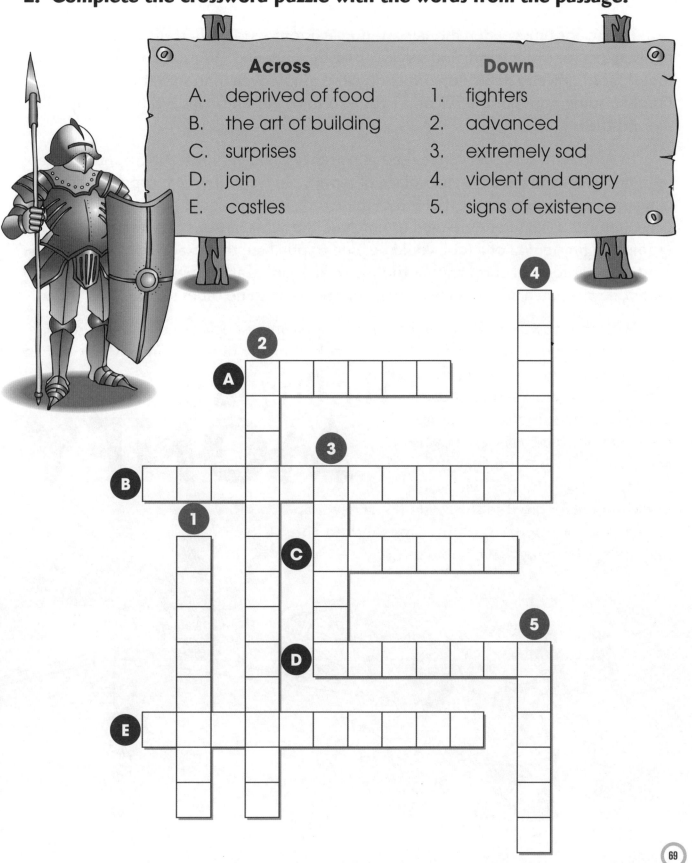

When we want to make a purchase today, we use money. We have many options as to how we pay with money. We can use a credit card, a debit card, a personal cheque, or cash.

In ancient times, when money was non-existent, people bartered (traded) goods and services for other goods and services that they needed. Items such as shells, beads, metal, gold, jewelry, feathers, and tools were always welcome in a trade. Instead of simply trading goods and services, a crude form of currency was established by tribes around the world.

In Africa and Asia, shells were used as currency while in North America, the Indians used necklaces and headdresses in place of money. In Central Africa, copper rods called congas were used as currency. For ten of these rods, a native could buy himself a wife. In China, bronze miniatures were used to purchase the actual articles they represented. For example, a tiny replica of a tool would be used to purchase that exact tool. Probably the most popular form of currency was the use of animals. Cattle, pigs, and camels are still used today to purchase products or make payments by some tribes in Asia.

With the growth of cities, standard forms of payment became necessary to regulate the value of goods. The barter method worked nicely between individuals or in a village setting, but it lacked consistency. There was no standard by which a person could measure the value of what they were buying. It was difficult to be sure that the deal was fair. Often the one who was the shrewdest dealer profited the most. It was necessary to establish a regular system. This marked the beginning of money as we know it today.

The Origins of MONEY

Remembering Facts and Making Assumptions

A. Answer the following questions based on the reading passage.

1.   Name four methods of payment we can use today.

a. _____   b. _____

c. _____   d. _____

2.   What does bartering mean?

_____

3.   Make a list of things that were used as currency in ancient times.

a. _____   b. _____

c. _____   d. _____

4.   Why was the use of bronze miniatures a clever way to make a purchase?

_____

_____

5.   Why do you think that animals were such a popular form of currency?

_____

_____

6.   Why was the bartering system not always fair?

_____

_____

Your Opinion

B. What skills would you need to possess to make you good at bartering?

1. _____

2. _____

3. _____

Rules of Capitalization

- Here are some rules to remember:

1. Use capitals at the beginning of sentences and questions.
2. Use capitals for all proper names and titles.
3. Use capitals for book and poem titles.
4. Use capitals for months of the year and special days.
5. Use capitals for brand names, company names, and religious terms.
6. Use capitals for names of countries, cities, lakes, rivers, and regions.

C. In the following passage, there are numerous words that should be capitalized. Change the small letters to capitals where necessary.

In fact, there are 42 capitals missing. Can you find them?

in the month of june, professor smith took jake and jordan, on a fishing trip up to moon river in the muskoka area of northern ontario. the drive from toronto took three hours but they stopped for lunch at mcdonald's. because the drive was so long, jordan brought his book entitled the best way to catch fish. he thought this book might help him learn how to fish. he was going to use the special fish hook called a surehook that he received for a birthday gift in may. it was made by acme fishing gear company located in montreal. when they arrived, they passed the old st. luke's church down the road from the river. working outside the church was pastor rodgers, who also likes to fish. he waved at them as they went by.

Haiku Poetry

- **Haiku Poetry** is a non-rhyming Japanese poem popular in the 19th century. It often dealt with nature as a theme.

- Haiku poetry consists of three lines with 5, 7, and 5 syllables in each line in that order.

  Example: Sun / surf / sand / and / sea   5 syllables

  Sail / boats / drift / ing / by / the /shore   7 syllables

  South / sea / wind / blow / ing   5 syllables

  The syllable breaks have been marked in the above poem. Notice that the poem is a collection of images (word pictures).

- Alliteration: **Alliteration** occurs when consecutive words begin with the same letter. In the poem above, there is sun, surf, sand, sea – all of which begin with the letter "s". Alliteration gives a poem a smooth rhythm and helps connect descriptive words and images.

D. Compose two Haiku poems. You may choose from the following topics or create your own. Try to use as many descriptive words as you can.

	Topics:	The Storm	Summer Morning
		Winter Night	Birds in Flight
		The Lion's Den	Children Playing

Title: _____

_____

_____

_____

Title: _____

_____

_____

_____

The interest in reaching the Far East through a northern passage was very high in Europe. The Spanish had <u>established</u> a <u>foothold</u> in South America and Mexico. The French and English, always <u>rivals</u>, were competing to <u>discover</u> a northern passage that would lead to China.

New France –
The Beginning Of Canada (1)

Francis I, king of France, selected Jacques Cartier to lead a voyage on a similar <u>route</u> to that taken by John Cabot in 1497. Cartier left France in 1534 with 2 ships and 60 men. In less than three weeks, he had crossed the Atlantic and reached Newfoundland. He <u>explored</u> the surrounding area known today as Prince Edward Island and New Brunswick. He erected a flag on Gaspé Peninsula and claimed the land for France. Cartier <u>convinced</u> an Indian chief named Donnaconna to allow him to take his two sons back to France in order to <u>impress</u> the king.

When he returned to France, Cartier was considered a hero. The king was so pleased with his efforts that he allowed for a second voyage. In 1535, Cartier set sail again with 3 ships and 110 men. When they reached the Gulf of St. Lawrence, the Indians returning with him led Cartier to the St. Lawrence River. Impressed by the size of the river, Cartier thought that the St. Lawrence River might lead to a passage to the East.

Continuing west down the St. Lawrence River, Cartier reached what is today Montreal. He named the village Mount Réal (Royal Mountain) in honour of the height of the mountain in the village. This was as far as Cartier could go because a short distance up the river, he came across rapids that were <u>impassable</u>. Cartier was forced to spend the winter there. He and his men were not prepared for the Canadian winter. They suffered <u>severe</u> cold, a <u>shortage</u> of food and supplies, and the <u>onset</u> of scurvy.

Examining Facts

A. Place "T" for true statements and "F" for false ones.

1. Europeans wanted a northern route to the East. _____

2. The Spanish had settlements in South America. _____

3. Cartier's route was different from Cabot's. _____

4. Francis I was king of France in 1534. _____

5. Cartier made it to Newfoundland in less than three weeks. _____

6. Cartier explored the area around P.E.I. and New Brunswick. _____

7. On his first voyage, Cartier left France with 200 men. _____

8. Cartier brought Indians back to France to impress the king. _____

9. Cartier took the sons of Donnaconna back to France. _____

10. Cartier was not interested in the St. Lawrence River. _____

11. Cartier visited a village which today is Montreal. _____

12. Cartier's voyage was stopped because of rapids. _____

B. Complete the chart to compare Cartier's two voyages.

		1st Voyage	2nd Voyage
1.	Date		
2.	Number of Ships and Men in the Crew		
3.	Important Accomplishments		

Punctuation: Commas and Quotation Marks

- Place **Quotation Marks** ("...") around the exact words spoken by a person.
  Example 1: Paul said, "I am going home now."
  Note: a comma is placed after the word "said" but not before it.
  Example 2: He said, "Good morning." Note: a comma is placed after "said".
  "Good morning," he said. Note: a comma is placed after "morning".

- Place a **Comma** between words in a series.
  Example 3: I like to eat potatoes, tomatoes, carrots, and beans.

- Special Note: Place a capital at the beginning of a quotation.

C. Punctuate the following sentences where necessary.

1. She screamed Look out

2. The teacher said Tonight for homework you have Math Science and Spelling

3. He played baseball soccer basketball and hockey

4. Let's go swimming said Janet to her friends

5. Linda yelled Is anyone there

Quotation marks are used to show people speaking or a dialogue. Another way of writing a dialogue is to list the speakers, each followed by a colon, and their speech. You do not need quotation marks in this case.

Example: John: How are you today, Paul?
          Paul: I'm fine. How are you?

D. Write a conversation between you and a friend. Place the speaker's name before the colon.

:	_____
:	_____
:	_____
:	_____

New Words in Context

- We can determine the meaning of a word by the idea behind the sentence in which it appears.

E.   Solve the crossword puzzles for the underlined words in the passage.

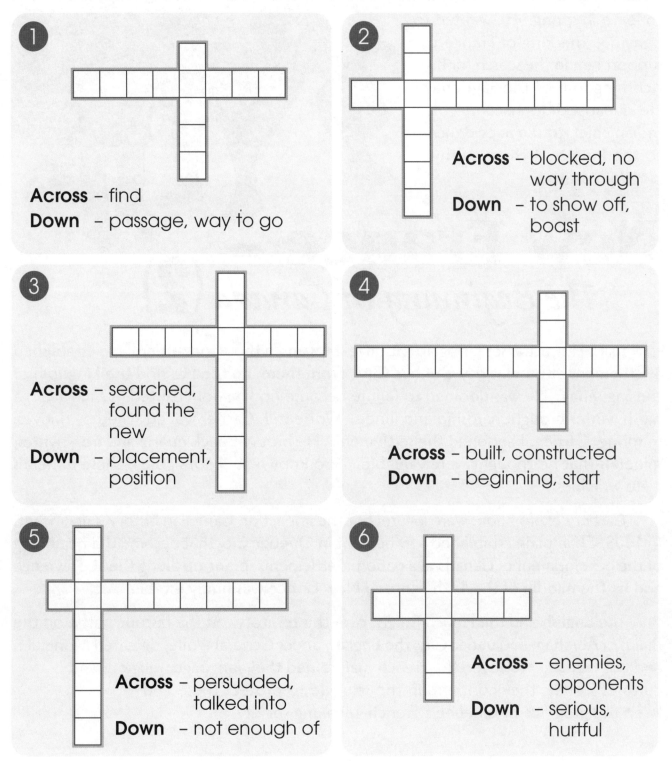

1

Across – find
Down – passage, way to go

2

Across – blocked, no way through
Down – to show off, boast

3

Across – searched, found the new
Down – placement, position

4

Across – built, constructed
Down – beginning, start

5

Across – persuaded, talked into
Down – not enough of

6

Across – enemies, opponents
Down – serious, hurtful

After the <u>miserable</u> winter of 1535, twenty-five of Cartier's men had died. Cartier <u>prepared</u> to leave in spring. He wanted to convince the king of France to support him in the search for the rich kingdom of the Saguenay. He kidnapped Donnaconna, the Indian chief, to use as evidence to the king that this wealthy kingdom existed.

New France –
The Beginning Of Canada (2)

In 1541, Cartier set sail again with five ships and a thousand <u>settlers</u>. He established a settlement at present day Quebec City. From there, he tried to find the kingdom of the Saguenay. He was doomed to <u>failure</u> because no kingdom existed. Once again a harsh winter brought <u>hardship</u> and illness. Worse still, Cartier was <u>attacked</u> by natives. In spring, Cartier abandoned the settlement. He brought back quartz and iron pyrites, minerals that he <u>thought</u> were valuable. Also known as "Fool's gold", these minerals were worthless.

Cartier's explorations were failures but the impact on Canadian history is significant. In 1608, Champlain established a settlement in Quebec City that became the beginning of the <u>development</u> of Canada as a nation. Settlements sprang up along the St. Lawrence and by the middle of the 17th century, New France was firmly established.

The English and the French <u>fought</u> over this territory. At the historic battle on the Plains of Abraham in Quebec City, the English, under General Wolfe, defeated Montcalm and the French. However, the French maintained their language, religion, and culture. Today, they continue in the struggle to protect these and keep the province of Quebec a French-speaking society.

Fact or Opinion

- A **Fact** is an exact statement given in the story. An **Opinion** is your personal point of view based on what you have read.

A. Place "F" for fact and "O" for opinion for each statement in the space provided.

1. Canadian winters can be harsh. _____

2. It is easier to travel in spring. _____

3. 25 of Cartier's men died. _____

4. Cartier thought there were riches in the Saguenay. _____

5. Cartier was cruel to Donnaconna. _____

6. Cartier wanted to prove to the king that there were riches in the Saguenay region. _____

7. Cartier was anxious to build a settlement. _____

8. There were no riches in the Saguenay region. _____

9. Quartz and iron pyrites could be used as jewelry. _____

B. In your opinion, was Cartier a success or a failure? Make a list of his successes and his failures in the chart below.

Accomplishments	Failures/Hardships
1.	1.
2.	2.
3.	3.

C. What natural wealth was there in Canada that Cartier overlooked?

_____

_____

Problem Sentences

• **Sentence Fragments**: *a sentence fragment is an incomplete sentence.*

   Example: *When I walk home from school...*
   This fragment needs more information for it to make sense.

   If you add "I see my friends on the way", then you would have:
   When I walk home from school, I see my friends on the way.

D.   Correct the following sentence fragments by adding the necessary information.

1.   During my lunch hour, _____ .

2.   After it stopped raining, _____ .

3.   _____ because the teacher asked.

4.   If it isn't too late, _____ .

5.   While I am watching television, _____ .

Combining Sentences

• Some sentences are too short. They are better when combined with another sentence that refers to the same topic.

   Example: It was Saturday morning. I woke up late.

   Could become: It was Saturday morning and I woke up late. or
   This Saturday morning, I woke up late.

E.   Combine the following short sentences.

Don't forget to use conjunctions.

1.   Carol called on Julie. Julie was not home.

_____

2.   Friday is a holiday. There is no school.

_____

3.   My teacher is nice. Mrs. Smith is my teacher. She teaches grade four.

_____

4.   Philip had a doctor's appointment. It was on Tuesday.

_____

Word Builder Crossword Puzzles

F. Each puzzle contains three root words for the underlined words in the reading passage. Use the clues to help you solve the puzzles.

Puzzle A

Puzzle A

Across – A. sadness
           B. get ready

Down – 1. make ready, calm, rest

Puzzle B

Across – A. form an idea
           B. build, make, form

Down – 1. firm, tough, difficult

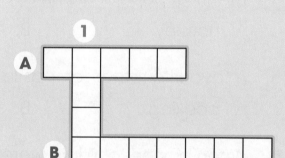

Puzzle B

Puzzle C

Puzzle C

Across – A. battle

Down – 1. not win
           2. charge

Review 2

Multiple Choice

A. **Circle the correct answer for each of the statements from the reading passages.**

1. The number of Harry Potter books sold is in the

   A. thousands.   B. millions.   C. hundreds.

2. Before writing her books, J.K. Rowling was

   A. very wealthy.   B. a struggling single mother.

   C. a housewife.

3. Pioneer children got their toys from

   A. making their own.   B. hardware stores.   C. trading posts.

4. The most popular game of pioneer times across Canada was

   A. hockey.   B. horseshoes pitching.   C. lacrosse.

5. A favourite father-son pastime in pioneer times was

   A. cooking.   B. sewing.   C. fishing.

6. When pioneer children weren't playing, they were

   A. doing chores.   B. sleeping.   C. watching television.

7. Early castles were not very comfortable because they were

   A. high on a hill.   B. too large.   C. cold and drafty.

8. The main purpose of a castle was

   A. to hold big parties.   B. to show wealth.   C. for protection.

9. The brain is the most important organ in the body because

   A. it is large.   B. it links to the nervous system.

   C. it helps us think.

10. The human brain stops growing when we are about

    A. 6 years old.   B. 18 years old.   C. 35 years old.

11. The human brain, when it is fully developed, weighs about

    A. 10 kg.   B. 25 kg.   C. 3 kg.

12. The Inca Empire ended when their territory was taken over by

    A. the French.   B. the Spanish.   C. the Portuguese.

13. The Inca built their cities on

    A. highlands.   B. flatlands.   C. cliffs.

14. Before the use of money, deals were made by

    A. guessing.   B. bartering.   C. arguing.

15. For trade in China, people used

    A. bronze miniatures. B. snakeskin.   C. furs.

16. Cartier returned to France with

    A. riches.   B. gold and jewels.   C. an Indian chief.

17. Cartier thought that riches lay in

    A. the Saguenay Region.   B. the St. Lawrence River.
    C. Montreal.

18. Cartier's men suffered from a disease called

    A. influenza.   B. scurvy.   C. smallpox.

19. Cartier attempted to build a settlement at present day

    A. Toronto.   B. Montreal.   C. Quebec City.

20. In 1608, a settlement in Quebec was established by

    A. King Francis I.   B. John Cabot.   C. Champlain.

Prepositions and Phrases

B. Add a suitable preposition in the space provided.

1. He hid _____ the table.   (under, through, inside)

2. She sunbathed _____ the backyard.   (under, into, in)

3. The dog ran _____ the yard.   (around, into, throughout)

4. The boat sailed _____ the river.   (into, down, between)

Phrases and Clauses

C. Write "P" if the underlined words are phrases or "C" if they are clauses.

1. <u>The purse on the bench</u> belonged to the old lady.   _____

2. I didn't go to Matt's party <u>because I was ill</u>.   _____

3. <u>Whenever they are free</u>, they play video games.   _____

4. The man <u>with a mustache on his face</u> is the manager.   _____

Adjective and Adverb Phrases

D. State whether the underlined words represent an adjective or an adverb phrase. Place ADJ or ADV in the space.

A phrase is a group of words introduced by a preposition that describes either a verb or a noun.

1. Go <u>into the garage</u> and get the lawnmower.   _____

2. The players <u>on the junior team</u> practise every day.   _____

3. The girls <u>in the class</u> sat <u>in the front</u>.   _____

4. <u>In the evening</u>, they watched a movie.   _____

5. The seat <u>in the front</u> cost much more money.   _____

Conjunctions

Conjunctions join other words, phrases, or main ideas in a sentence.

E. **Underline the conjunctions in the following sentences.**

1. It may taste bad but it's good for you.

2. She will not be late if she leaves on time.

3. Either Joe or Paul will be captain of the team.

4. It was overcast although the forecast was for sunny weather.

Capitalization and Punctuation

F. **Correct the missing capitals in each sentence. Add proper punctuation.**

1. mr. smith asked john to meet him at lions stadium

2. she said could someone please assist me

3. lauren and kara read a judy blume story

4. peaches plums pears and nectarines are expensive in winter

5. he shouted let me in it's cold outside

Types of Sentences

G. **State whether the following sentences are declarative, imperative, interrogative, or exclamatory and punctuate them accordingly.**

1. Get up, you're going to be late _____

2. Who will help with the work _____

3. Wow _____

4. This is the main street in town _____

Review 2

H. Match the words from the passages with the definitions.

1.	vital	_____	A. searched, looked into
2.	responsibility	_____	B. imaginative
3.	amazing	_____	C. serious, dangerous
4.	complex	_____	D. unknown
5.	creative	_____	E. enemies
6.	mystery	_____	F. important
7.	rivals	_____	G. duty
8.	explored	_____	H. not enough
9.	severe	_____	I. complicated, numerous
10.	shortage	_____	J. surprising, unbelievable

I. Complete the sentences with the correct form of the given words.

1. Yesterday Paul (laugh) _____ when he heard the joke.

2. The sun shone on the (beauty) _____ flowers.

3. The bird was (chirp) _____ loudly.

4. Crossing the road can be (danger) _____ .

5. She was (perform) _____ in the school play.

6. They lived (happy) _____ ever after.

7. He made a (donate) _____ to the charity.

8. Being on time proved that she was (rely) _____ .

86

9.   The puppy was very (life) _____ .

10. The children were (terrify) _____ by the scary movie.

 Forming New Words

J.   Choose the proper prefix for each of the following words.

1.   sincere   in, un   : _____

2.   direct   in, de   : _____

3.   patient   un, im   : _____

4.   belief   dis, un   : _____

5.   known   non, un   : _____

6.   proper   un, im   : _____

7.   behave   mis, dis   : _____

8.   certain   dis, un   : _____

9.   believable   un, im   : _____

 **Plurals**

K.   Write the proper plural form of the following words.

1. hero		2. army	
3. city		4. lady	
5. life		6. leaf	
7. half		8. tomato	
9. goose		10. mouse	

Answers

1 Ghosts

A. 1. T 2. F
   3. T 4. T
   5. F 6. T
B. 1. B 2. C
   3. D 4. A
C.   (Individual answers)
D. 1. cried 2. tired
   3. find 4. hears
   5. behave 6. walked
   7. delicious 8. ran
E. 1. stadium 2. singer
   3. school 4. tower
   5. car
F. 1. E 2. C
   3. J 4. G
   5. I 6. H
   7. B 8. D
   9. A 10. F
G.   (Individual writing)

2 The Human Heart

A. 1. D 2. B
   3. C 4. C
   5. A
B. 1. E 2. A
   3. B 4. C
   5. F 6. D
C. 1. flew ; A 2. played ; A
   3. is ; N 4. were ; N
   5. is ; N 6. sang ; A
   7. was ; N 8. cross ; A
D. 1. went 2. flew
   3. sailed 4. camped
   5. built 6. stayed
   7. took
E.

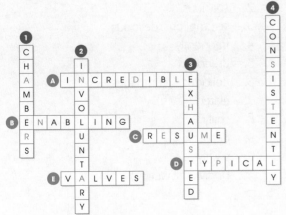

3 The First Heart Transplant

A. 1. O 2. F 3. F 4. O
   5. F 6. F 7. O 8. F
   9. F 10. O 11. O 12. O
B.   (Individual writing)
C. 1. excited ; loud
   2. tall ; husky ; heavy
   3. shiny ; new ; red ; perfect ; birthday
   4. tired ; warm
   5. expensive ; top ; antique
D. 1. never
   2. silently ; quickly
   3. gallantly
   4. proudly ; brilliantly
   5. bravely ; courageously
E. 1. its 2. cloths
   3. here 4. dairy
   5. feat 6. fourth
   7. dual 8. weather
   9. dessert 10. loose
F.   (Individual writing)

4 The Incredible Butterfly

A. 1. They have beautiful colours.
   2. They pollinate plants when they feed.
   3. Some use their colour as camouflage while others use their bright colour as a warning. The Magnificent Owl butterfly's large dot on its wing makes predators think that it is a much larger animal.
B. 1. egg 2. larva
   3. pupa 4. adult
C. 1. nectar 2. proboscis
   3. flowers 4. pupa
   5. world 6. Magnificent Owl
   7. Monarch
D. 1. She ; it 2. mine
   3. he 4. they
   5. theirs 6. it
   7. them
E. 1. Which 2. Who
   3. Whose 4. What
   5. Which
F. 1. exchange ; changeable
   2. imprint ; printing
   3. impolite ; politeness
   4. disbelieve ; believable

Answers

5. impatient ; patience
6. unreal ; realistic
7. indefinite ; definitely
8. misbehave ; behaviour
9. disappoint ; appointment
10. insincere ; sincerity

G.
1. transformation
2. warning
3. creations
4. widest
5. diversity
6. tropical
7. beautiful
8. depending

5 The Atlas

A.
1. G
2. E
3. D
4. F
5. H
6. J
7. I
8. A
9. C
10. B

B. (Order may vary.)
1. Atlantic
2. Pacific
3. Indian
4. Arctic
5. Antarctic

C. Australasia ; Asia ; Europe ; Africa ;
South America ; North America ; Antarctica

D.
1. brother
2. cabinet
3. tennis
4. me
5. papers
6. thief
7. passengers
8. breakfast ; school
9. dress ; shoes
10. clouds ; flowers

E. (Individual writing)

F.
1. entire
2. globe
3. circles
4. exact
5. scale
6. prime

G. (Individual writing)

6 Disasters at Sea (1)

A.
1. B
2. B
3. B
4. C

B. (Individual writing)

C.
1. dog
2. me

3. Cathy
4. mechanic
5. him
6. mother
7. him

D. (Individual writing)

E.
1. many
2. disasters
3. left
4. expensive
5. fancy
6. large
7. saw
8. fell

F. (Individual writing)

7 Disasters at Sea (2)

A.
1. F
2. T
3. F
4. F
5. T
6. F
7. T
8. F
9. T
10. F

B.
1. May 30, 1914 ; May 7, 1915 ; November 21, 1916
2. passenger ship ; luxury ship ; hospital ship
3. St. Lawrence River ; Southern coast of Ireland ; Mediterranean Sea
4. collided with another ship ; torpedoed ; hit a mine or torpedoed
5. 14 minutes ; 18 minutes ; 55 minutes
6. 1012 ; 1195 ; 30

C.
1. He | played
2. parents | told
3. presents | were
4. friend | is
5. two | make
6. They | played

D.
1. D
2. E
3. A
4. B
5. C

E.
1. elegant
2. spacious
3. scrumptious/delicious
4. frequently
5. drenched
6. delicious/scrumptious
7. elated
8. chilly
9. depressing
10. swiftly

F. (Individual writing)

8   Plants – Nature's Medicine

A. 1. G   2. E
    3. F   4. B
    5. C   6. D
    7. H   8. A
B. 1. T   2. F
    3. F   4. T
    5. T   6. F
    7. T   8. F
    9. T
C. (Individual writing)
D. (Individual writing)
E.
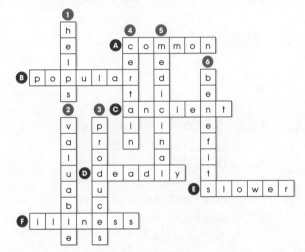

9   Education in the Renaissance

A. (Individual answers)
B. 1. The birthday cake had nine candles on it.
    2. The cat chased the mouse around the room.
    3. The father and his son went fishing in the lake.
    4. School began when the summer holidays ended.
C. (Individual answers)
D. (Individual writing)
E. (Individual writing)

Review 1

A. 1. T   2. F
    3. F   4. T
    5. F   6. F
    7. T   8. F
    9. T   10. T
    11. T   12. F
    13. T   14. F
    15. F   16. T
    17. T

B. 1. C   2. B
    3. A   4. C
    5. B   6. A
    7. C   8. A
    9. C   10. A
    11. B
C. 1. (likes) ; ice cream ; day
    2. (tripped) ; shoelace ; (fell) ; stairs
    3. boys ; girls ; (played) ; yard
    4. Jim ; John ; Sam ; (walked) ; school
    5. Linda ; (is) ; years ; Susan
    6. neighbours ; (held) ; sale ; street
    7. Winter ; (is) ; season
    8. Time ; (is wasted) ; (do) ; nothing
    9. clock ; (struck) ; bell ; (rang)
D. 1. blazing ; (slowly)
    2. happy ; birthday ; (quickly)
    3. (Slowly) ; (surely) ; skilled
    4. tall ; (immediately) ; basketball
    5. (swiftly) ; stone ; sandy
E. 1. her   2. She
    3. me   4. They
    5. she
F. 1. (me) ; ball
    2. (Grandma) ; postcard
    3. (son) ; bicycle
    4. (running back) ; ball
    5. (us) ; chance
G. 1. D   2. A
    3. B   4. C
    5. E
H. 1. B   2. I
    3. J   4. A
    5. D   6. C
    7. G   8. E
    9. H   10. F
I. 1. diary   2. fourth
    3. feat   4. whether
    5. duel   6. hear
J. (Suggested answers)
    1. arrangement   2. disorganized
    3. preview   4. disconnect
    5. remind   6. disappoint
    7. dissatisfied 8. creative
    9. disbelief   10. careful
    11. reliable   12. dependable
    13. distance   14. unhappy
    15. priority   16. unknown

Answers

K.
1. delicious
2. hilarious
3. bitterly
4. kind
5. drenched ; pelting
6. spacious ; antique

10 J.K. Rowling – Her Story

A. B ; B ; C ; B
B. (Individual writing)
C. (Individual writing)
D.
1. un   2. dis
3. un   4. im
5. im   6. dis
7. dis   8. un
9. un   10. in
11. un   12. im
E.
1. kindness
2. terribly
3. careful
4. movement
5. celebration
6. helpful
7. beautiful
8. solution

11 Games and Toys of Pioneer Canada (1)

A. (Individual answers)
B. (Individual writing)
C.
1. sky   2. morning
3. pond   4. school
5. rain
D.
1. moon   2. tuffet
3. hill   4. wall
5. clock
E. (Individual writing)
F. (Individual writing)

12 Games and Toys of Pioneer Canada (2)

A.
1. a stuffed pig's bladder
2. a pigskin
3. hoop rolling
4. a silhouette
5. dolls
6. a tree branch
7. no automobiles
B.
1. O   2. O

3. O   4. F
5. F
C.
1. P   2. C
3. P   4. P
5. C   6. C
7. P   8. C
D. (Individual writing)
E.
1. star   2. canoe
3. pot   4. peach
5. cloud
F.
1. wear   2. hear
3. threw   4. mane
5. weak   6. sail

13 Medieval Castles

A.
1. B   2. B
3. A   4. A
5. C   6. C
B.
1. (In the morning) ; (over the cliffs)
2. of grade four ; (at his desk)
3. in the kennel
4. (under the desk)
5. (up the road) ; (down the hill)
6. (Under the rainbow) ; of gold
C. (Individual writing)
D.
1. knives
2. lives
3. halves
   "f" or "fe" to "ves"
4. armies
5. families
6. cities
   "y" and add "ies"
7. journeys
8. keys
9. valleys
   "s"
E.
1. geese   2. children
3. feet   4. men
5. teeth   6. mice
7. The singular and plural are the same in spelling.

14 The Thinking Organ

A.
1. organ
2. growing
3. process
4. memory

5.   emotions
6.   cerebrum
7.   cerebellum
8.   left
9.   hypothalamus
10. nervous

B.   1.   E   2.   D
     3.   B   4.   C
     5.   F   6.   A

C.   (Individual answer)

D.   1.   and   2.   unless
     3.   since   4.   because
     5.   or   6.   while
     7.   but   8.   if
     9.   so   10. until

E.   1.   complex
     2.   dominant
     3.   amazing
     4.   organs
     5.   mystery
     6.   emotions
     7.   connected
     8.   fear
     9.   vital
     10. creative
     11. function
     12. stored

F.   (Individual writing)

15   The Inca Empire

A.   1.   T   2.   T
     3.   T   4.   T
     5.   T   6.   T
     7.   F   8.   T
     9.   F   10. F

B.   1.   The Inca were able to build their cities and
          fortresses on highlands and steep slopes, with
          stone steps leading up to the top of the cities.
     2.   (Individual answer)
     3.   They fought the Inca warriors with guns.

C.   1.   ! ; Excl.   2.   . ; Imp.
     3.   . ; Decl.   4.   ? ; Int.
     5.   . ; Imp.

D.   (Individual writing)

E.

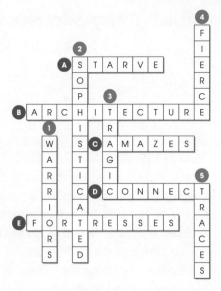

16   The Origins of Money

A.   (Suggested answers)
     1a. credit card   b.   debit card
     c.   cheque   d.   cash
     2.   It means trading.
     3a. shells   b.   feathers
     c.   tools   d.   jewelry
     4.   The item being used for currency directly
          represented the item being purchased.
     5.   They could be killed for food or used for work.
     6.   The shrewdest trader profited the most.

B.   (Individual writing)

C.   In the month of June, Professor Smith took Jake
          and Jordan, on a fishing trip up to Moon River in
          the Muskoka area of Northern Ontario. The drive
          from Toronto took three hours but they stopped
          for lunch at McDonald's. Because the drive was
          so long, Jordan brought his book entitled The Best
          Way To Catch Fish. He thought this book might
          help him learn how to fish. He was going to use
          the special fish hook called A Surehook that he
          received for a birthday gift in May. It was made
          by Acme Fishing Gear Company located in
          Montreal. When they arrived, they passed the
          old St. Luke's Church down the road from the
          river. Working outside the church was Pastor
          Rodgers, who also likes to fish. He waved at them
          as they went by.

D.   (Individual writing)

Answers

17   New France – The Beginning of Canada (1)

A. 1. T   2. T
    3. F   4. T
    5. T   6. T
    7. F   8. T
    9. T   10. F
   11. T   12. T

B. 1. 1534 ; 1535
    2. 2 ships and 60 men ; 3 ships and 110 men
    3. Explored P.E.I. and New Brunswick ; claimed land for France ; brought back Donnaconna's sons ; Reached Montreal ; named village Mount Réal

C. 1. She screamed, "Look out!"
    2. The teacher said, "Tonight for homework, you have Math, Science, and Spelling."
    3. He played baseball, soccer, basketball, and hockey.
    4. "Let's go swimming," said Janet to her friends.
    5. Linda yelled, "Is anyone there?"

D.   (Individual writing)

E. 1.   2.

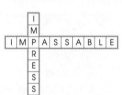

    3.   4.
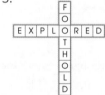

    5.   6.
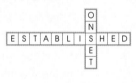

18   New France – The Beginning of Canada (2)

A. 1. O   2. O
    3. F   4. F
    5. O   6. F
    7. O   8. O
    9. O

B.   (Individual answers)

C.   (Suggested answer)
        He overlooked the furs of the woodland animals such as foxes and beavers.

D.   (Individual writing)

E. 1. Carol called on Julie but Julie was not home.
    2. Because Friday is a holiday, there is no school.
    3. My grade four teacher, Mrs. Smith, is nice.
    4. Philip had a doctor's appointment on Tuesday.

F.   Puzzle A

        Puzzle B
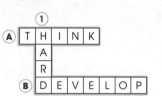

        Puzzle C

Review 2

A. 1. B   2. B
    3. A   4. B
    5. C   6. A
    7. C   8. C
    9. C   10. A
   11. C   12. B
   13. A   14. B
   15. A   16. C
   17. A   18. B
   19. C   20. C

B. 1. under   2. in
    3. around   4. down

C. 1. P   2. C
    3. C   4. P

D. 1. ADV   2. ADJ

94

　　3. ADJ ; ADV 　　　　4. ADV
　　5. ADJ
E. 1. but 　　　　　　　2. if
　　3. or 　　　　　　　4. although
F. 1. Mr. Smith asked John to meet him at Lions Stadium.
　　2. She said, "Could someone please assist me?"
　　3. Lauren and Kara read a Judy Blume story.
　　4. Peaches, plums, pears, and nectarines are expensive in winter.
　　5. He shouted, "Let me in! It's cold outside."
G. 1. Get up, you're going to be late. ; imperative
　　2. Who will help with the work? ; interrogative
　　3. Wow! ; exclamatory
　　4. This is the main street in town. ; declarative
H. 1. F 　　　　　　　　2. G
　　3. J 　　　　　　　　4. I
　　5. B 　　　　　　　　6. D
　　7. E 　　　　　　　　8. A
　　9. C 　　　　　　　10. H
I. 1. laughed
　　2. beautiful
　　3. chirping
　　4. dangerous
　　5. performing
　　6. happily
　　7. donation
　　8. reliable
　　9. lively
　　10. terrified
J. 1. insincere
　　2. indirect
　　3. impatient
　　4. disbelief
　　5. unknown
　　6. improper
　　7. misbehave
　　8. uncertain
　　9. unbelievable
K. 1. heroes
　　2. armies
　　3. cities
　　4. ladies
　　5. lives
　　6. leaves
　　7. halves
　　8. tomatoes
　　9. geese
　　10. mice